FIGHT THE GOOD FIGHT

75 DAYS
OF GROWING CLOSER TO JESUS

TINA C. ELACQUA, PH.D.
WITH LISA GUEST, M.A.

WESTBOW
PRESS®
A DIVISION OF THOMAS NELSON
& ZONDERVAN

This book is a work of nonfiction. Unless otherwise noted, the author and the publisher make no explicit guarantees as to the accuracy of the information contained in this book and in some cases names of people and places have been altered to protect their privacy.

WestBow Press books may be ordered through booksellers or by contacting:

WestBow Press
A Division of Thomas Nelson & Zondervan
1663 Liberty Drive
Bloomington, IN 47403
www.westbowpress.com
844-714-3454

Because of the dynamic nature of the Internet, any web addresses or links contained in this book may have changed since publication and may no longer be valid. The views expressed in this work are solely those of the author and do not necessarily reflect the views of the publisher, and the publisher hereby disclaims any responsibility for them.

All Scripture quotations, unless otherwise indicated, are taken from the New Revised Standard Version, Updated Edition. Copyright © 2021 National Council of Churches of Christ in the United States of America. Used by permission. All rights reserved worldwide.

Scripture quotations marked (ESV) are from The Holy Bible, English Standard Version. ESV® Text Edition: 2016. Copyright © 2001 by Crossway Bibles, a publishing ministry of Good News Publishers.

Scripture quotations marked (NIV) are from Holy Bible, New International Version®, NIV® Copyright ©1973, 1978, 1984, 2011 by Biblica, Inc.® Used by permission. All rights reserved worldwide.

Scripture quotations marked (NLT) are from Holy Bible, New Living Translation, copyright © 1996, 2004, 2015 by Tyndale House Foundation. Used by permission of Tyndale House Publishers, Inc., Carol Stream, Illinois 60188. All rights reserved.

Scripture quotations marked (NKJV) are from the New King James Version®. Copyright © 1982 by Thomas Nelson. Used by permission. All rights reserved.

Any people depicted in stock imagery provided by Getty Images are models, and such images are being used for illustrative purposes only. Certain stock imagery © Getty Images.

ISBN: 979-8-3850-3106-1 (sc)
ISBN: 979-8-3850-3107-8 (e)

Library of Congress Control Number: 2024916094

Print information available on the last page.

WestBow Press rev. date: 09/05/2024

Everything… is worthless when compared with the
infinite value of knowing Christ Jesus my Lord.
Philippians 3:8 (NLT)

DEDICATION

For my beloved girls, Hannah Maria and Christina: May you continue to walk in God's love and light.

For my dearly loved mother, Maria Cannistraci Elacqua: You were instrumental in my getting to know Jesus and building a life-giving relationship with Him.

For Sharla Walstrom and Kelley Schmidt: You invested in me and discipled me, teaching a young Tina that a truly fulfilling life happens only when a genuine relationship with Jesus as both Savior and Lord is our foundation.

And for you who were guided by the Spirit to pick up this book: May He use it to awaken in you the desire to know—or know better—the one and only Jesus and to deepen your intimacy with Him through whom all things are possible.

FOREWORD

Do you know Jesus?

Do you long for a more intimate relationship with Jesus?

Do you want to finish well this race of life?

Having recently entered my retirement years, I've been reflecting on my life—on how God has worked in me and is still working in me as well as on how I want to live out my remaining years. I don't want, for instance, to become apathetic and lazy, neglecting my gifts and ignoring my God-given purpose. Yes, I can enjoy a slower pace, but I long to continue serving and growing in my relationship with my Savior and Lord. I also pray that God will use me for His kingdom work until the day He takes me home. Perhaps that's your prayer too.

If so, I hope that, like me, you can find a role model in Paul: he lived his life to the fullest, acting in response to God's call until he took his last breath. Paul started out rough—as in, he persecuted God's people—but he was transformed when he recognized Jesus as Lord and surrendered everything to Him. Paul served God throughout his days no matter what hardship he encountered. At the end of my life, I want to be able to say, as Paul did, "I have fought the good fight; I have finished the race; I have kept the faith" (2 Timothy 4:7).

As long as we're on this earth, we have a God-given purpose: we are to share the good news about Jesus and to love people with His love. Furthermore, God continues to work in us, transforming our lives until that day we see Him face-to-face.

In *Fight the Good Fight: 75 Days of Growing Closer to Jesus,* my friend Dr. Tina Elacqua masterfully guides us through the life of Paul and highlights his spiritual transformation. As she does so, Tina is transparent about the difficult experiences in her own life that could have kept her from following God and staying the course. Speaking with a heart of someone who knows firsthand what it's like to face adversity, she desires to spur women on in their walk with God and to encourage them when they're struggling. Her love for Christ kept Tina from quitting. Instead, that love enabled her to press on in obedience to Jesus just as Paul did. She challenges us to do the same.

Every devotion in *Fight the Good Fight* invites us to experience a closer intimacy with Jesus and shows us the life change that comes as we lean into Him who holds us close through every challenge and hardship we face.

I highly recommend this devotional book for all believers and those who seek to believe, especially those who desire to become more like Jesus and long to finish well. You won't be disappointed.

Crickett Keeth
Bible study author and former Director of Women's Ministry
www.crickettkeeth.com

INTRODUCTION

I am so glad you picked up this book—and I'm so excited about the ways the Holy Spirit might use it in your life to help you know Jesus better. That's my purpose in putting together these 75 devotions: I pray that you will come to know Jesus—or know Him better—as we look at the life and ministry of Paul, an apostle of Jesus Christ and the writer of many of the faith-building and life-giving New Testament epistles.

When we meet this first-century Jew, he is a prime candidate for Jerusalem's "Most Likely to *Never* Follow Jesus" award. In the Bible's initial mention of him, we see the then-called Saul witnessing and approving the stoning of Stephen, a man devoted to Jesus, whom he believed to be the long-awaited Messiah. We also read that "Saul was ravaging the church, and entering house after house, he dragged off men and women and committed them to prison" (Acts 8:3 ESV).

Yet this is the man whom God used to establish churches, disciple fellow believers, share the gospel with the Gentiles, set forth theological truth, and offer real-life encouragement to honor and glorify God in all we do. How did this transformation from murderer to evangelist happen? And can that kind of transformation from persecutor to a person on fire for the Lord happen to you?

The book you hold in your hands will not only answer that first question one day at a time, but it can also serve as a tool to help you yourself experience the Saul-to-Paul transformation from merely knowing *about* Jesus to knowing Jesus more intimately than you do now. Facilitating that transformation is the Challenge that comes at the end of each devotion. I encourage you to take a few minutes to, in response to that prompt, apply or wrestle with or celebrate the truth that the day's passage and devotion set forth.

As you get to know your Lord more intimately through this study of His Word, you'll begin to speak, think, and act more like Him. As you yield to His power, the Holy Spirit will transform you into a winsome witness for Jesus.

May *Fight the Good Fight: 75 Days of Growing Closer to Jesus* also reassure you of Jesus' deep love for you. He who died on the cross for your sin longs for you to know Him more intimately. You can be confident that He is walking this journey through Acts and Paul's New Testament epistles with you. Don't hesitate to slow down along the way to listen for His voice of love. After all, it is the love of Jesus that will empower you to fight the good fight, living with the eternal prize of heaven in your sights and walking in the grace and strength of your Savior and Lord (see 1 Timothy 6:11–12).

God bless your travels toward a richer relationship with Jesus.

Tina

DAY 1

KNOWING ABOUT VS. KNOWING

I regard everything as loss because of the surpassing value of knowing Christ Jesus my Lord.
Philippians 3:8

Do you know Jesus?

Or do you just know *about* Jesus?

Consider the vast difference between the two options. The first implies relationship and heart connection; the second, merely head knowledge. The first option—actually knowing Jesus—means a richer, more significant life here on earth as well as eternal life. Knowing about Jesus may help you move toward that life-giving relational knowledge, but if it doesn't, that knowledge is no more useful than acknowledging with a "So what?" shrug of the shoulders that exercise is good for you but remaining a couch potato.

So when I say, "Do you know Jesus?" I'm asking if you've entered into a relationship with Him. Do you spend time with Jesus? Are you committed to loving Him, obeying Him, and honoring Him with your life? Do you seek greater intimacy with Him? Are you fighting "the good fight of the faith," fleeing ungodliness and pursuing "righteousness, godliness, faith, love, endurance, gentleness" (1 Timothy 6:11–12)?

A Jewish man named Saul couldn't have answered yes to these questions. Oh, Saul knew *about* Jesus—and hated Him. Saul hated everything about Jesus, including His followers, those Christians who knew Jesus intimately and walked through life with Him.

Where do you stand? Are you a Saul, a person who knows *about* Jesus, but doesn't love Him and isn't concerned about obeying Him? Perhaps, like Saul, you are a persecutor of Christians, snubbing them, mocking them, belittling them, discriminating against them, slandering them, gossiping about them, or lying about them? Or have you rejected Jesus Himself, throwing up your hands before Him and saying, "I don't want anything to do with You!" Or maybe, prompted by discouragement rather than anger, you've just given up on God?

If you want to know Jesus rather than just know *about* Him, you can be sure that He very much wants you to know Him. For more details about getting to know Jesus as Savior and Lord—the way Saul did—turn to "The Romans Road to Salvation" at the back of this book.

Challenge: What might you do this week to walk more closely with the Lord? Go to church? Open your Bible every morning? Make time to pray?

DAY 2

GOD-EMPOWERED FORGIVENESS

"Blessed are you when people revile you and persecute you and utter all kinds of evil against you falsely on my account."
Jesus in Matthew 5:11

Saul hated Christians and persecuted them, tracking down men and women alike and throwing them into prison. After his conversion, he admitted, "I persecuted the followers of this Way to their death" (Acts 22:4 NIV). And what were all these people guilty of? Being followers of Jesus.

In Jerusalem, this hard-hearted Saul witnessed the death of Stephen, a man "full of grace and power" who had performed great works and signs among the people (Acts 6:8). Stephen also spoke with great wisdom that stirred jealous listeners to "secretly instigate" lies about him (Acts 6:11). These false accusations led to Stephen's arrest and an appearance before the Jewish Council where he boldly preached the gospel, ending with the accusation that these religious leaders had "betrayed and murdered" the Righteous One, the long-awaited Messiah (Acts 7:52 ESV).

Before the first stone was thrown, though, Stephen gazed into heaven and proclaimed, "I see the heavens opened and the Son of Man standing at the right hand of God" (Acts 7:56). Enraged, some of the listeners rushed toward Stephen, dragged him outside the city, and began their murderous assault.

Yet, as the stones struck his body, this man of faith cried out with a loud voice, "Lord, do not hold this sin against them" (Acts 7:60). Just as his Savior, Jesus Christ, had done from the cross, Stephen asked God to forgive these men who took his life.

Standing in the circle as the stones crushed Stephen's body, Saul "approved of their killing him" (Acts 8:1). The Greek word translated *approved* means "took pleasure with others." Saul and his fellow persecutors took pleasure in the wrongful and brutal death of Stephen.

Challenge: When, if ever, have you been wrongly accused? Can you be like Stephen and ask God to extend grace to those accusers? Why or why not?

DAY 3

JESUS' HIGH STANDARD

"If you forgive others their trespasses, your heavenly Father will also forgive you, but if you do not forgive others, neither will your Father forgive your trespasses."
Jesus in Matthew 6:14–15

Chances are, you haven't met a cold, heartless man who could witness the death of an innocent person and remain unmoved. Not only did Saul say nothing as Stephen was stoned to death, but he left the site of the murder even more intent on "ravaging the church" (Acts 8:3).

Tragically, I *have* encountered a man like Saul, alive in body, but dead in spirit. That man was guilty of the cold-blooded first-degree murder of my parents. My anger was real and my grief, profound. This loss brought a whole new level of pain.

But the Holy Spirit had been at work in my heart. Like many of you, I'd long held on to anger and bitterness from various hurts. I knew I needed to forgive—and I wouldn't do it. But at one point, by God's grace and mercy, I recognized the Lord's conviction, received His grace for my sinful unforgiveness, and yielded to His transforming power. The Lord enabled me to forgive. Because Jesus had done this work, I was walking in a life of forgiveness when my parents were murdered. That's not to say I didn't feel indescribable anger and pain, but by God's grace, I arrived relatively quickly at the place of forgiveness.

Yes, the murder of my parents tested me to the core. But by

God's grace and the Holy Spirit's power, I was able to do what Stephen did: I asked God to not hold this man's sin against him. God enabled me to forgive the murderer . . . and I did so again and again as I grieved the loss of my parents. Nothing is impossible with God.

Challenge: Whom, if anyone, do you need to forgive? Whether the offense happened yesterday or twenty years ago, why are you carrying around a burden of bitterness, anger, and hate? Spend some time with the Lord who calls you to forgive.

TINA C. ELACQUA, PH.D.

DAY 4

HOW MANY TIMES?

*If you, L*ORD*, kept a record of sins, Lord,
who could stand?*
Psalm 130:3 (NIV)

My ability to forgive my parents' murderer was the result of our gracious God's work in my heart. He gets all the credit and all the glory for not only enabling me to forgive but also for teaching me about forgiveness. I learned a biblical model of forgiveness, and it's based on Jesus' parable of the unforgiving debtor in Matthew 18:21–35.

First, a quick summary of Jesus' story. A servant owed the king 10,000 talents—and a talent was worth about 20 years of a laborer's wages. The servant fell before the king and begged for more time to pay his debt. Relenting, the merciful king actually forgave the servant the entire debt. That servant, however, then encountered someone who owed him far less, 100 denarii, the wages of a hundred days of work. This servant—forgiven a far greater debt—did *not* extend forgiveness for this much smaller debt. When the gracious king learned of this injustice, he was furious and threw this servant into prison.

What prompted Jesus to tell this story? His disciple Peter had asked the Lord, "If my brother or sister sins against me, how often should I forgive? As many as seven times?" (v. 21). Jesus responded, "Not seven times, but, I tell you, seventy-seven times" (v. 22). We aren't to keep a tally of how often we've forgiven someone just as God Himself doesn't keep a tally of how often He forgives us. Rather than being based on some mathematical formula, forgiveness is a matter of the heart.

Challenge: Which is easier: keeping a tally of how many times we've forgiven someone, or drawing near to God so He can keep our heart soft and enable us to extend the grace of forgiveness? Why do we, like Peter, want to know exactly how much mercy we need to extend? In light of the parable, why is that concern ludicrous?

DAY 5

AGAIN AND AGAIN
AND AGAIN

"Forgive us our debts, as we also have forgiven our debtors."
Jesus in Matthew 6:12

Forgiveness is a matter of the heart, but that doesn't mean we sit around and wait for feelings of forgiveness to descend. We are to take action based on what Jesus teaches us about forgiveness, based on the biblical model of forgiveness I offer in these pages.

First, Jesus tells us that forgiveness is to be ongoing. We are to forgive the person who hurt us and then forgive that person again and again, every time we find ourselves feeling anger and hate for that person. The depth of the wound determines how often we will be forgiving that injury or loss.

Whomever you need to forgive or forgive again—a spouse, significant other, parent, child, friend, acquaintance, colleague, sister, brother, relative, someone who has passed, perhaps someone who hasn't even asked for forgiveness—do so. God will help you forgive or forgive again. There is no limit to the number of times we are to extend forgiveness for a single wound. We are to forgive as many times as we need to.

Second, as the king in Jesus' parable demonstrated at the start of the story, forgiveness is merciful, and we who have been mercifully forgiven are to mercifully forgive others. After all, the sin which you and I are guilty of cost Jesus His life, yet He is faithful to forgive us for whatever our sin and whenever we ask (1

John 1:9). Certainly we can extend a fraction of that mercy to the people in our life.

Challenge: Be honest with God about where you are struggling to extend mercy and forgiveness. A lack of forgiveness can lead to bitterness, cynicism, and worse. God wants to help you be free of that burden.

DAY 6

A MATTER OF OBEDIENCE

The love of God is this, that we obey his commandments.
And his commandments are not burdensome.
1 John 5:3

His body mangled and bleeding, Jesus nailed to the cross is a picture of God's grace: we certainly don't deserve having the Sinless One take on the punishment for our sins. This God-given favor is completely undeserved and unmerited. Yet, in His grace and mercy, Jesus died so we can know His forgiveness. But the forgiveness doesn't stop there. He commands us to then extend forgiveness to those people who have hurt us.

Simply put, forgiveness is a matter of doing what God commands. Paul, for instance, wrote, "Just as the Lord has forgiven you, so you also must forgive" (Colossians 3:13) and "Be kind to one another, tenderhearted, forgiving one another, as God in Christ has forgiven you" (Ephesians 4:32). And Jesus concluded His parable about the unforgiving servant with a warning for those who don't obey the command to forgive: "So my heavenly Father will also do to every one of you [throw you into prison], if you do not forgive your brother or sister from your heart" (Matthew 18:35).

God issues that command because He doesn't want us to be in a spiritual prison of unforgiveness. He wants us to know freedom from that burden; He wants us to know an abundant life and freedom in Him. Key to experiencing that is extending forgiveness again and again, mercifully, and in obedience to God. He truly will help us forgive our debtors as we have been forgiven our debts.

Challenge: Have you noticed that all of God's commands are for our own good? Think of a handful of examples. Now consider what is good for us about the command to forgive those who offend, hurt, or harm us. Be specific about a few of the ways we benefit from forgiving.

TINA C. ELACQUA, PH.D.

DAY 7

WHAT EXACTLY IS FORGIVENESS?

"If you do not forgive others, neither will your Father forgive your trespasses."
Jesus in Matthew 6:15

Look again at that hard truth Jesus spoke. In light of that statement, we would do well to understand what forgiveness is and what it isn't. Over the next handful of days, we're going to look at five key aspects of forgiveness that will, I pray, enable you to forgive more freely.

First, forgiveness means *freeing yourself from bondage* to the person who offended you. In Luke 4:18, Jesus came to set prisoners free, and we make ourselves prisoners when we choose unforgiveness rather than forgiveness.

Picture a ball and chain. That iron ball connected to your ankle by a heavy chain is anyone who has offended, hurt, or harmed you—and who may be completely oblivious to that connection between the two of you. I'm sure my parents' murderer never considered how he might be haunting me after their death. But thoughts of this evil man definitely weighed me down—until I decided that I didn't want to be chained to him. This murderer had taken away my parents, but I wouldn't let him take anything else from me, especially not my physical and spiritual health. He would have stolen my health, though, if I'd chosen to stay chained to him.

When you and I forgive, we cut loose the offender. We no longer drag him around, and we can know the freedom Jesus promised us.

Will you choose the life of freedom you'll find when you forgive or the heavy burden of darkness and despair?

Challenge: Identify any ball and chain keeping you from knowing the freedom of forgiving. Have you been betrayed by a friend, cheated on, lied to, gossiped about, backstabbed, or physically, emotionally, verbally, sexually, or spiritually abused? Perhaps you've been impacted by someone's alcohol or drug abuse. I pray you haven't experienced the murder of a loved one. Whatever the ball(s) and chain(s) in your life, will you cut loose the offender(s) from you? Why or why not?

DAY 8

DO WHAT?

*Bless those who persecute you. Don't curse
them; pray that God will bless them.*
Romans 12:14 (NLT)

Last time, we discussed the first of five key aspects of biblical
forgiveness. We realized that when we forgive, we cut ourselves
loose from the offender whose action has weighed us down. We
find that we are the prisoner Jesus sets free from the ball and chain
of unforgiveness.

Forgiveness also means we *pray for the offenders.* Jesus Himself
said, "Love your enemies and pray for those who persecute you"
(Matthew 5:44). As we've recognized, all God's commands are for
our good, and I can attest to the good that comes from praying for
a person you need to forgive. You see, God uses the prayer time
you spend with Him to work in your heart. Praying for the one
you need to forgive will change that person's hold on your heart.
I know that for a fact.

I experienced an amazing change in my heart once I began
praying for the man who murdered my parents. I went from anger
and rage to compassion, mercy, and Christ's love. In fact, I found
myself wanting to give this murderer a Bible, explain the gospel
of Jesus Christ, and tell him I forgave him.

I am so grateful for God's transformative work in my heart—
and I know He longs to do the same for you. Will you start praying
today for God to "bless those who persecute you"? You'll probably

just be going through the motions at first, just saying the words but not really meaning them. But you'll soon be grateful for the change of heart God gives you.

Challenge: What keeps you from praying for your enemy, for the person you need to forgive? Consider what the Lord who loves you would say about each of those reasons.

TINA C. ELACQUA, PH.D.

DAY 9

"FATHER, FORGIVE THEM"

"Father, forgive them, for they do not
know what they are doing."
Jesus in Luke 23:34

We've looked at two aspects of forgiveness—freeing ourselves from the offender's hold on us and praying for that person—but do we take those steps *even if that person hasn't asked for our forgiveness*? The short answer is yes, as our Lord and Savior showed us.

As He hung dying on the cross, experiencing excruciating pain with every breath He struggled to take, Jesus strained to speak these words about the soldiers who were overseeing His crucifixion: "Father, forgive them, for they do not know what they are doing" (Luke 23:34). Jesus' murderers hadn't had a change of heart since nailing Him to the cross; asking to be forgiven was the furthest thing from their mind.

Earlier, some Roman soldiers had flogged Jesus, put on Him a crown of thorns, and jeered at Him with the cry, "Hail, King of the Jews!" (John 19:3). The soldiers at the cross had brutally hammered nails into Jesus' hands and feet, mocked Him with the sign "The King of the Jews" (John 19:19) and gambled for His clothes. Despite such cruel treatment, Jesus said, "Father, forgive them."

The truth is, we can—as our Savior did—forgive the offending person without being asked to do so. After all, Jesus forgave the Roman soldiers without being asked. He also suffered the capital punishment that would ensure the forgiveness of our sins without our asking Him to do so.

Back to the matter of us extending forgiveness. If we had to wait for the offender to ask for our forgiveness, we'd be placing ourselves back in bondage to that person. We'd be reattaching the ball and chain. And what if that request for forgiveness never came?

Forgiveness means forgiving even when the offender has not asked to be forgiven.

Challenge: Why do we want our offenders to ask us to forgive them? What heart business, if any, do you need to take up with God in light of your answer?

TINA C. ELACQUA, PH.D.

DAY 10

FORGIVENESS IS NOT APPROVAL

Never avenge yourselves, but leave room for the wrath of God, for it is written, "Vengeance is mine; I will repay, says the Lord."
Romans 12:19

We human beings can be very good at finding reasons we don't want to do things, even things that are good for us, even things that God commands. As we've seen, forgiving people who have offended and hurt us can prompt in us many reasons (excuses?) not to do exactly that. Remember "But they haven't asked for forgiveness"?

I've also heard many hurting people say, "If I forgive my offender, I'm saying that what she did is OK." That is simply not true. The gossip, the stealing, the unfaithfulness, the cruel words, or the irrational actions were bad and wrong, hurtful and unfair. That point will rarely be argued. John Miles's murdering my parents is not OK and will never be OK. My choice to forgive that heartless man will *never* make what he did OK.

Rather than indicating any kind of approval, our choice to forgive is instead an act of freeing ourselves from the person who hurt us. We act in obedience to God when we forgive, and obeying His commands is always good for us.

We therefore need to accept the truth that our forgiveness is not a commentary on a person's actions or words. Oh, Satan wants you to believe that extending forgiveness is condoning that person's wrong against you, but Satan is a liar.

The truth is, when we forgive, it does *not* make the offense OK. Forgiving makes *you* OK.

Challenge: What do you think is the source of this idea that forgiving means we approve of the wrong done against us? Why might some of us struggle to accept the truth that forgiving is *not* condoning? What truth can you use to counter the lie that forgiving means that what was done was OK?

TINA C. ELACQUA, PH.D.

DAY 11

FORGIVE AND FORGET?

*"I will be merciful toward their iniquities, and
I will remember their sins no more."*
Hebrews 8:12

Today we look at the final truth in our five-point biblical perspective on forgiveness. First a quick review of the first four.

1. When we forgive, we free ourselves from the offender's hold on us.
2. God changes our heart as we pray for the person who hurt us.
3. We don't wait for the offender to ask to be forgiven before we start this forgiving and praying-for process.
4. We remind ourselves as often as necessary that forgiveness is not approval of the hurt or offense.

Finally, when we forgive, *we don't need to forget.* And based on my own experience, I can say wholeheartedly that this reality is a good thing,

You see, I have chosen to not bury the pain that came when my parents were murdered. I've chosen the healthy but difficult option of feeling a hurt so profound that I didn't know I could hurt that much. To be honest, I will always be grieving the loss of my parents, and I will never forget that heinous act that ended their lives and changed mine forever.

Even though I won't ever forget the murders, I also don't think about them all the time. As I've traveled this journey toward forgiving the murderer, God has taught me and enabled me to discipline my mind and focus on Christ and on whatever is true, honorable, just, pure, pleasing, commendable, excellent, and worthy of praise (see Philippians 4:8).

The Lord wants you to not always be thinking about your wounds and sorrows. He wants to give you rest. At the same time, know that God is a righteous Judge: you can trust Him to judge the person who hurt you.

Challenge: Today's verse talks about God "remembering our sin no more." Do you think this means that He completely forgets our sins and/or that He no longer dwells on them and He will never hold them against us? Explain your thinking and what you learn from this verse.

DAY 12

FIVE ASPECTS OF FORGIVENESS

"If the Son makes you free, you will be free indeed."
Jesus in John 8:36

Over the last several days, we have learned a lot about what the Bible teaches about forgiveness.

- Forgiveness is an ongoing process, and we are to forgive a sin as many times as we need to in our journey to freedom from the anger or hurt.
- Forgiveness is merciful. When we forgive someone, we refrain from acting on our anger and our ideas about what consequences that person deserves. Our choice not to act is simultaneously an extension of grace: we are giving that person the unmerited favor of forgiveness, an undeserved gift to ourselves as well as to the offender who escapes our revenge.
- God commands forgiveness: because God forgives me, I am to forgive others.

In addition to these basic truths, we've looked at five aspects of biblical forgiveness in an attempt to define *forgiveness* and determine what forgiving means and doesn't mean.

- Forgiving means choosing to not be in bondage to the offender, but rather allowing Jesus to set us free.

- Forgiveness means praying for the offender and finding that God changes our heart when we go before Him in humility.
- We forgive even when the offender has not apologized, much less asked to be forgiven.
- Forgiving never makes the offense OK, but it makes us OK.
- When we forgive an offense, we don't need to forget about it. But we trust God to righteously judge the offender.

When we receive God's forgiveness and when we forgive others, we enjoy a life of freedom and abundant peace and joy. Go forth, my friends, and live a life of forgiveness!

Challenge: Which basic truth about forgiveness and/or which aspect of biblical forgiveness was most significant for you? Why? What action steps, if any, has this section on forgiveness prompted you to take? Spend a few minutes thanking God for His forgiveness and for what He's taught you about forgiveness, but don't stop there. Ask Him to bring to mind anyone you need to forgive—and then do so.

DAY 13

BEST-LAID PLANS

The human mind plans the way,
*but the L*ORD *directs the steps.*
Proverbs 16:9

As we've seen, the very first scene in the story of Saul's post-conversion transformation offers us a portrait of forgiveness. That practice is so key to our relationship with Jesus as well as our relationships with the people in our life that we spent a lot of time on that topic. Now we're back to the Jewish man named Saul who watched the stoning of Stephen and perhaps heard the martyr pray and ask God to forgive his murderers.

Saul knew about Jesus—and hated with a white-hot passion this itinerant Teacher as well as those Jews who had begun to follow Him as their Rabbi. This respected Pharisee "was ravaging the church" after Stephen's death, dragging men and women off to prison (Acts 8:3). Then, wanting to expand his reach to Damascus, Saul—"breathing threats and murder against the disciples of the Lord" (Acts 9:1)—received permission from the high priest to bind any Christian men and women he found and take them back to Jerusalem.

Yet as Saul walked toward Damascus, a light from heaven suddenly flashed around him. Stunned, he fell to the ground and heard a voice saying, "Saul, Saul, why do you persecute me?" He asked, "Who are you, Lord?" The reply came, "I am Jesus, whom you are persecuting" (see Acts 9:3–5). Imagine what Saul thought and felt! And what a wild way to begin moving from merely knowing about Jesus to *knowing* Him.

Jesus continued: "Get up and enter the city, and you will be told what you are to do" (Acts 9:6). Jesus had not only Saul's attention, but also a life-changing purpose for this Christian-persecuting Jew.

Challenge: Whether you recognized it in the moment or when you looked back, reflect on how a change in your plans or the direction you were heading was clearly the work of God. What was the impact of that divine intervention on the trajectory of your life? What was its impact on you spiritually?

TINA C. ELACQUA, PH.D.

DAY 14

FROM BLINDNESS TO SIGHT

The god of this world has blinded the minds of the unbelievers, to keep them from seeing clearly the light of the gospel of the glory of Christ, who is the image of God.
2 Corinthians 4:4

As he walked the road to Damascus with his entourage, set on persecuting followers of Jesus, Saul was not the only one who heard the voice say, "Saul, Saul, why do you persecute me?" (Acts 9:4). The men Saul was traveling with heard the voice, too, but they didn't see anyone speaking. They were stunned and speechless... until Saul stirred.

Rising from the ground, Saul had his eyes open, but he saw nothing. All these men had, however, heard the voice command, "Get up and enter the city, and you will be told what you are to do" (Acts 9:6). The men therefore guided their blind leader by the hand to the destination city of Damascus and to the unknown "what you are to do" awaiting them.

For three days Saul "was without sight and neither ate nor drank" (Acts 9:9). What might Saul have thought and felt at this point? I'm sure he was relieved that his traveling companions had also heard the voice whose instructions he was following. The experience had to have been quite unsettling, prompting Saul to question his convictions. The followers of Jesus were wrong and should be persecuted as betrayers of the Jewish faith, right? These people who had abandoned the ancient Jewish ways deserved death, didn't they? Saul's encounter with Jesus must have made him wonder....

Perhaps there was more to this Jesus of Nazareth, reportedly crucified but raised from the dead, than Saul had realized.

Challenge: The circumstances probably weren't as dramatic as Paul's road-to-Damascus experience, but reflect on the moment you recognized Jesus as God's Son and committed your life to Him. What sin did you abandon after realizing you needed to change your ways? What wrong ideas did you replace with truth?

DAY 15

WE DON'T KNOW WHAT
WE DON'T KNOW

*I count everything as loss because of the surpassing
worth of knowing Christ Jesus my Lord.*
Philippians 3:8 (ESV)

Saul experienced three days of blindness after his encounter
with the risen Jesus. Before that physical blindness, though, and
unbeknownst to him, Saul had been spiritually blind. That past
confidence revealed his ignorance about the gospel:

> I, too, have reason for confidence in the flesh...:
> circumcised on the eighth day, a member of the
> people of Israel, of the tribe of Benjamin, a Hebrew
> born of Hebrews; as to the law, a Pharisee; as to
> zeal, a persecutor of the church; as to righteousness
> under the law, blameless. (Philippians 3:4–6)

Saul knew that pleasing God meant obeying His commands,
and Saul had become an expert in both knowing exactly what the
law required and acting in obedience. His sincere desire to live in
a way that honored God fueled in him a passion that led him to
persecute the radical followers of Jesus. In His compassion, God
stopped Saul in his tracks and taught him the gospel truth.

I want to be sure you know the gospel truth. First, God's Word
tells us that every single one of us has sinned (Romans 3:23),

and the spiritual consequence of our sin is death (Romans 6:23), meaning separation from God now and for eternity. But by God's grace, the gospel story doesn't end there.

Jesus—God's Son who was completely without sin (1 Peter 2:22)—came into this world and died on the cross. When Jesus gave Himself to die as the sacrifice for our sins, He paid for your sin and mine, enabling us to live in relationship with our holy God now and for eternity. If you haven't already, will you accept this gift of forgiveness and eternal life?

Challenge: If you're a believer, what wrong ideas about Christianity did you once have? Thank God for enabling you to recognize His truth. If you aren't yet a follower of Jesus, who could answer any questions you have about Christianity so you can be rid of any wrong ideas?

TINA C. ELACQUA, PH.D.

DAY 16

A MESSENGER TO THE GENTILES

*"Go therefore and make disciples of all nations,
baptizing them… and teaching them to obey
everything that I have commanded you."*
Jesus in Matthew 28:19–20

We've asked how this miraculous transformation from murderer of Christians to preacher, evangelist, church planter, and New Testament writer happened. Well, it started when, as Saul traveled to Damascus, he met Jesus.

A bright light shined down from heaven, Saul fell to the ground, and he heard a voice call him by name and ask, "Why do you persecute me?" (Acts 9:4). Understandably Saul wanted to know who was asking this question. In response, Jesus identified Himself, but He didn't stop there. Jesus told Saul, "Get up and enter the city, and you will be told what you are to do" (Acts 9:6).

Saul gave more details about this command when he later told King Agrippa of Judea about his road-to-Damascus conversion experience. The disembodied voice had indeed said, "Get up and stand upon your feet," but Saul offered further details:

> "Get up and stand on your feet, for I have appeared to you for this purpose, to appoint you to serve and testify to the things in which you have seen me and to those in which I will appear to you. I will rescue

you from your people and from the gentiles—to whom I am sending you to open their eyes so that they may turn from darkness to light and from the power of Satan to God, so that they may receive forgiveness of sins and a place among those who are sanctified by faith in me." (Acts 26:16–18)

Pause to consider what Saul might have been thinking and feeling when he heard that divine job description, issued by the Lord Himself.

Challenge: Look again at the assignment Jesus gave Saul. What aspects of that job seem unlikely for this Christian-persecuting Pharisee? What is Jesus' job description for you? (Hint: see Matthew 28:19–20 above.) What aspects of that job seem unlikely, uncomfortable, or difficult for you? Would God command you to do something He won't enable you to do? Explain your answer.

DAY 17

FEAR NOT!

Be strong and courageous. Do not be frightened,
and do not be dismayed, for the LORD your
God is with you wherever you go.
Joshua 1:9 (ESV)

When, if ever, has God called you to do something that sounded irrational or even dangerous? Today we're going to meet Ananias, who would indeed have a story to tell in response to that question.

Ananias was a disciple of Jesus Christ living in Damascus when the Lord interrupted his daily life with a vision. Hearing the Lord call his name, Ananias responded, "Here I am, Lord" (Acts 9:10), and that's when God gave him a specific and radical assignment: "Get up and go to the street called Straight, and at the house of Judas look for a man of Tarsus named Saul" (Acts 9:11).

Saul of Tarsus? Ananias was well aware of this murderous Pharisee. Concerned about his safety, Ananias reminded God of the evil Saul had done in Jerusalem and was authorized to do in Damascus. In response to Ananias's reservations, God described Saul as "an instrument... I have chosen to bring my name before gentiles and kings and before the people of Israel" (Acts 9:15).

Reassured if not also startled by the sovereign goodness of this assignment, Ananias obeyed God. Arriving at the house where Saul was, Ananias explained that he had been sent by the same Lord Jesus whom Saul had seen on the road to Damascus. Laying his hands on Saul, Ananias prayed, and Saul regained his vision.

Then His immediate baptism was a public proclamation of the inner transformation of his heart from murderer to evangelist.

I like to imagine the Lord saying to Ananias, "Well done, good and faithful servant."

Challenge: When, if ever, has God called you to do something irrational, seemingly impossible, or even dangerous? Is He calling you right now to do something that sounds impossible? Perhaps reaching out to someone you think will never accept the truth about Jesus Christ? Know that God will honor your obedience just as He honored Ananias's.

DAY 18

GROWING YOUR RELATIONSHIP WITH JESUS

As you therefore have received Christ Jesus the Lord,
continue to walk in him, rooted and built up in him and
established in the faith... abounding in thanksgiving.
Colossians 2:6–7

After Saul's conversion and the baptism that declared his commitment to Jesus, this new follower of Christ spent three years in Arabia (see Galatians 1:17–18). During that time, Saul grew in his understanding of the gospel and how Jesus fulfilled the Old Testament teachings he knew so well. But Saul didn't grow only in his knowledge about Jesus; Saul came to better know Jesus Himself.

After those three years in Arabia, Saul spent a couple weeks with Peter before going on to Syria and Cilicia (see Galatians 1:18, 21). As Saul put it, "I was still unknown by sight to the churches of Judea that are in Christ; they only heard it said, 'The one who formerly was persecuting us is now proclaiming the faith he once tried to destroy.' And they glorified God because of me" (Galatians 1:22–24).

You and I didn't spend time in Arabia or fifteen days with Peter cementing our relationship with Jesus. But consider your own spiritual growth: What church did you get involved in shortly after becoming a believer? What sources of knowledge (books, Bible studies, sermons) were most significant to you? Which fellow followers of Jesus were key to your growth in your faith? Think about God's hand in the initiation and the growth of your relationship with Jesus Christ—and thank Him.

Challenge: What are you currently doing to grow in your relationship with Jesus Christ? Are you worshiping regularly... building relationships with a community of Jesus followers... spending some time each day reading, studying, and meditating on God's Word... participating in a Bible study or Sunday school class... and talking to the Lord as you would a friend (aka praying)? May the Lord Jesus Christ bless you as you come to know Him better and better.

DAY 19

A NEW CREATION

If anyone is in Christ, [she] is a new creation.
The old has passed away; behold, the new has come.
2 Corinthians 5:17 (ESV)

After Saul's conversion and mysterious three-year education in Arabia, he returned to Damascus (Galatians 1:17). Consider the significance of that.

The enraged Saul had been heading to Damascus—a trip of 150 miles—to arrest and drag back to a Jerusalem prison any men and women who were following Jesus instead of making Jewish tradition and the long-revered Mosaic law their priority. But what was this persecutor of Jesus' followers doing now?

We see in Acts 9:20 (NIV) that Saul was preaching in the Damascus synagogues, and his message was simple and straightforward: "Jesus is the Son of God." People who recognized Saul would not have expected that teaching from him:

> All who heard [Saul] were amazed and said, "Is not this the man who made havoc in Jerusalem among those who invoked this name [Jesus]? And has he not come here for the purpose of bringing them bound before the chief priests?" (Acts 9:21)

We read in the next verses that Saul grew more effective in his presentation of the message that Jesus is the long-awaited Messiah—and it wasn't long before some of the Jews of Damascus were plotting to kill him. Whose side was this renowned Pharisee on anyway? How could Saul teach ideas that undermined their Jewish ways and threatened their faith as well as their way of life?

Besides, even if his message had been acceptable, how could Saul the preacher once have been Saul the persecutor?

Challenge: If you're a Christian, know that the testimony of a life changed because of an encounter with Jesus Christ is worth sharing. Think about who you were BC (before you met Jesus) and how you are different today. What personal trait do you see as the most significant aspect of the new creation you are in Jesus?

DAY 20

WE ALL NEED A BARNABAS

Encourage one another and build one another up.
1 Thessalonians 5:11 (ESV)

Having escaped from the Damascus Jews who wanted to murder him, Saul headed to Jerusalem. There he encountered in Jesus' disciples the same fear and concern the Jews of Damascus had felt. It makes complete sense that the disciples "were all afraid of him, for they did not believe that he was a disciple" (Acts 9:26). What would convince them?

In His gracious design, God sent Saul an advocate named Barnabas, a Levite and native of Cyprus. The Jerusalem Christians originally knew him as Joseph, but later named him Barnabas, meaning "son of encouragement" (Acts 4:36).

I love that the word *encouragement* has the word *courage* in it, and that word also describes Barnabas quite well. He was quite courageous to befriend Saul when this persecutor-turned-believer returned to Jerusalem. No one besides Barnabas seemed to believe he was truly a follower of Jesus. Other Christians undoubtedly thought Saul was trying to trick them into confessing they were Jesus followers so he could arrest them, put them in chains, and drag them before the chief priests.

Barnabas, however, courageously took a chance: he chose to trust Saul, the two became friends, and Barnabas later introduced Saul to his brothers and sisters in Christ. Because of Barnabas, Christians in Jerusalem saw that Saul was no longer a murderer, but an evangelist; no longer zealous for the law, but zealous for Jesus Christ.

Challenge: Who has been a Barnabas in your life? Who has encouraged you in your faith, welcomed you into a Christian community, and/or stood with you when you didn't want to stand alone in your beliefs? Thank God for that person—and consider thanking that person! Also ask the Lord to show you who in your life needs you to be a Barnabas and reach out to that person with some encouragement.

DAY 21

ANOTHER KIND OF ENCOURAGEMENT

*You will be enriched in every way so that you can
always be generous. And when we take your gifts
to those who need them, they will thank God.*
2 Corinthians 9:11 (NLT)

Barnabas, "son of encouragement," surely did not limit his kindness and support to Saul alone. The Christian community had undoubtedly benefited from Barnabas' selfless, courageous, and encouraging ways. After all, they were the ones who started calling him Barnabas!

We find evidence, for instance, that Barnabas exercised his gift of encouragement in Acts 4 when he "sold a field that belonged to him, then brought the money and laid it at the apostles' feet" (v. 37). This statement comes at the end of a description of the early Christian community who "were of one heart and soul, and… everything they owned was held in common" (v. 32). Luke, the author of the book of Acts, reported that God poured "great grace" on His people, and no one among them lacked for anything they needed (v. 33). In fact, "as many as were owners of lands or houses sold them and brought the proceeds of what was sold and laid it at the apostles' feet, and it was distributed to each as any had need" (vv. 34–35 ESV).

Barnabas did exactly that. This respected leader of the church generously used his gifts—his material possessions as well as his ability to encourage people with his actions and words—to serve the Lord and further His kingdom work.

Challenge: Everything we have—our time, talents, abilities, skills, money, home, and the list goes on—belongs to the Lord. Spend some time thanking the Lord for all that He has entrusted to you and asking Him to show you with what He wants you to be more generous. Whether it's finances, time, skills, and/or your home, may you be like Barnabas and share generously.

TINA C. ELACQUA, PH.D.

DAY 22

THE GENTILES? REALLY?

*Is God the God of Jews only? Is he not the God
of gentiles also? Yes, of gentiles also.*
Romans 3:29

We meet up with encouraging and generous Barnabas again in Acts 11. Upon learning that Gentiles in Antioch had become believers, the church in Jerusalem sent Barnabas to, I'm sure, encourage these people who had recently named Jesus their Savior and Lord:

> When [Barnabas] came and saw the grace of God,
> he rejoiced, and he exhorted them all to remain
> faithful to the Lord with steadfast devotion, for he
> was a good man, full of the Holy Spirit and of faith.
> And a great many people were brought to the Lord.
> (vv. 23–24)

Not everyone who learned of the Gentiles' conversion was as joyful as Barnabas. Having grown up knowing they were God's chosen people, the ones to whom He would send the Messiah, many faithful Jews struggled when they heard about Gentiles accepting the truth about who Jesus was. This paradigm shift—this radical idea that non-Jews were to be welcomed into the community of God's chosen people—was too huge for them to manage on their own.

Clearly, the Lord Himself—by the power of the Holy Spirit—needed to work in their minds and hearts to remove their prejudice against Gentiles so they would accept these new believers as brothers and sisters in Christ and, later, accept Saul's ministry to them. Jesus cares about your soul, not about your race, social position, economic status, gender, or denomination. In His church—in the body of believers—"There is no longer Jew or Greek; there is no longer slave or free; there is no longer male and female, for all… are one in Christ Jesus" (Galatians 3:28).

Challenge: Whom do you struggle to welcome into the fellowship of believers? What person walking into your church sanctuary on a Sunday morning would you have a hard time greeting warmly and inviting to sit with you? Confess that to God and ask Him to work in your mind and heart so that you can love all fellow believers with His love.

DAY 23

OUR REDEEMER GOD

To all who mourn in Israel,
he will give a crown of beauty for ashes,
a joyous blessing instead of mourning,
festive praise instead of despair.
Isaiah 61:3 (NLT)

Saul has come a long way since Acts 7 when he witnessed the stoning of Stephen. On that day, Acts 8:1 says, Saul was part of "a severe persecution... against the church in Jerusalem, and all except the apostles were scattered throughout the countryside of Judea and Samaria."

Later, Saul found himself needing to flee Jerusalem. He had gone there after his conversion, been befriended by Barnabas, and begun boldly preaching the truth about Jesus. Among those who heard Saul were Greek-speaking Jews who, after arguing with him, plotted to kill him. The man whose action had prompted many Jews to flee Jerusalem after the death of Stephen now found himself needing to flee that same town to preserve his own life.

Consider, however, that the Lord used the Acts 8:1 scattering of believers to facilitate the spread of His gospel. In fact, our Redeemer God specializes in bringing good out of bad (Romans 8:28). God used these uprooted Jewish Christians to grow His kingdom. The tragic loss of their homes, jobs, routines, and fellowship of believers meant eternal life for people who had never heard about Jesus.

I'm guessing you've seen this same Redeemer God bring good out of something awful in your life. I'm still grieved by the murder of my parents, but God has used my suffering to draw me into a more intimate relationship with Jesus. He has also used my tragedy to give me opportunities to invite others to know my Lord and Savior, Jesus Christ. To Him be the glory!

Challenge: Describe how God has redeemed pain, loss, or tragedy in your life. If you're not sure, ask Him to open your eyes and show you. And perhaps you're wondering what, if anything, God can do to redeem some current circumstances. Ask Him to help you trust that He will use your pain for your good and His glory.

TINA C. ELACQUA, PH.D.

DAY 24

LIFELONG DISCIPLESHIP

You will grow as you learn to know God better and better.
Colossians 1:10 (NLT)

Remember how thrilled Barnabas was to learn that God had welcomed Gentiles of Antioch into His kingdom of faith? Upon arriving in that town, Barnabas saw clear evidence of the grace of God, and he rejoiced.

Barnabas, a man of God fighting "the good fight of the faith" (1 Timothy 6:12) and "full of the Holy Spirit and of faith," also headed to Tarsus, Saul's hometown, to invite Saul to partner in this Antioch ministry (Acts 11:24–26). Those new believers didn't have the foundation of Jewish history, law, and tradition that Jewish Christians did. They needed to be discipled, and Barnabas apparently believed God had equipped Saul for such a task.

The term *disciple* has a Latin root, meaning "learner" or "pupil/student." The goal of being a disciple or student of Jesus is to learn whatever we don't know but need to know to live a life that honors God. So we study God's Word. There, we discover who the Lord is and how to live out the truth of Scripture, our love for Jesus, and His love for us. This discipling happens when we intentionally spend time with God's people, when we regularly study the Bible, and when we consistently hear it preached. Ideally, as we get older, we find ourselves in the role of discipler and have the privilege of teaching others about our Savior and Lord.

Know that our role as disciple never changes. At any point of our life, when we sit at the feet of Jesus, we always learn more.

Challenge: In what ways are you being a disciple of Jesus? What, for instance, are you doing to be a student of God's Word—or what could you do? In what ways are you involved in your church? What opportunities to be with God's people do you regularly make time for? At what time of day do you spend some time with the Lord, praying and maybe journaling? Also, be aware of opportunities to be a discipler even as you continue to be a disciple yourself.

DAY 25

BEARING JESUS' NAME

"Let your light shine before others, so that
they may see your good works
and give glory to your Father in heaven."
Jesus in Matthew 5:16

I love thinking of myself as a disciple of Jesus Christ—and I hope that's true for you. Being His disciple means being His student. It means being able to draw near to Jesus, to ask Him questions, to rely on His Holy Spirit to help me understand truth, and to know not only more about Him, but also to know Him better. How amazing it is to have as our Teacher the One who created the world, who gave His life to pay our sin-debt, and who has proved victorious over death. Being His student also keeps me mindful of my purpose in life: to know Him well so I may teach others about Him.

Another term I use to describe myself—a term that ranks right up there with the word *disciple*—is *Christian*. Followers of Jesus were first called Christians in the city of Antioch (Acts 11:26). As the Holman Christian Standard Bible explains they earned that name because their behavior, activities, and speech reflected the behavior, activities, and speech of Jesus Christ Himself. What a compliment, you might think, but this term was probably first used to mock or ridicule these believers in Christ.

Today, the term *Christian* can mean far worse than mockery or ridicule. It can mean persecution and even death. Perhaps you've felt a bit threatened or at least very alone at the workplace or a social event when someone comments on your faith. Perhaps you've encountered discrimination at your job or strained relationships in your family.

I hope the apostle Peter's words encourage you: "If any of you suffers as a Christian, do not consider it a disgrace, but glorify God because you bear this name" (1 Peter 4:16).

Challenge: Think about how open you are—or aren't—about your commitment to Jesus. How do you respond when family, friends, neighbors, or colleagues comment on or challenge your faith? What would you like your response to be?

TINA C. ELACQUA, PH.D.

DAY 26

SO WHO IS THIS HOLY SPIRIT?

It is no longer I who live, but it is Christ who lives in me.
Galatians 2:20

In the introduction to this book, you met Saul, the persecutor of Christians. As the account of Acts unfolds, you'll continue to see his radical transformation into Paul, the preacher whom God used—and still uses today—to save souls for Jesus. The key to Paul's transformation is the Holy Spirit who came into his heart the moment he acknowledged his need for a Savior and recognized Jesus as the Savior whom God had provided. As Paul would one day write, "Christ... lives in me." If you're a believer, Christ also lives in you by the Spirit's indwelling presence.

So who is this Holy Spirit who lives in believers? The Holy Spirit is the third Person of the Triune God who exists as Father, Son, and Holy Spirit, Three as One. Equal to God the Father and Jesus the Son, the Holy Spirit is all knowing (1 Corinthians 2:10), all powerful (Acts 1:8), and present everywhere (Psalm 139:7). The Holy Spirit empowers us believers to do the kingdom-of-God work we have been called to do (1 Corinthians 12:4–11).

Consider some specific aspects of the Spirit's unique role in the life of believers: He is, for instance, our Advocate or Helper (John 16:7); our Teacher (1 Corinthians 2:12–13); and the Spirit of Truth (John 16:13). The Spirit prays for us (Romans 8:26); comforts us (Acts 9:31); leads us (Romans 8:14; Galatians 5:16); convicts us of our sin (John 16:8); and calls to mind biblical words of truth when we need them (John 14:26). The prophet Isaiah described the spirit of the Lord as "the spirit of wisdom and understanding, the spirit of counsel and might, the spirit of knowledge and the fear of the LORD" (11:2).

Everyone who welcomes Jesus as Savior and Lord receives the Holy Spirit, but not all of us believers are fully yielded to the Spirit. After all, we have the moment-by-moment choice to turn away from our human nature and instead turn to the Holy Spirit and submit to His influence, guidance, and transformative power. When we yield all of ourselves—body, mind, spirit, soul—to the Holy Spirit, we experience the fruit of His presence within us: We find ourselves more able and willing to love selflessly and sacrificially. We both experience and exhibit joy, peace, patience, kindness, goodness, faithfulness, gentleness, and self-control, all due to the presence of the indwelling Spirit of Jesus.

Challenge: Spend a few moments thanking God for the gift of His Holy Spirit. Then think about a time when the Holy Spirit worked in your life in one of the specific ways mentioned in the third paragraph. Despite experiences like the one you just shared, what tends to keep you from being fully yielded—body, mind, spirit, soul—to the Holy Spirit? What is one specific step you can take toward being more yielded to Him?

TINA C. ELACQUA, PH.D.

DAY 27

ACCOUNTING FOR YOUR HOPE

Always be ready to make your defense to anyone who
demands from you an accounting for the hope that is in you,
1 Peter 3:15

Saul accepted Barnabas's invitation to serve with him among the new believers in Antioch. The two of them spent a year there discipling those who had put their faith in Jesus as the Messiah, as their Savior (Acts 11:26).

Imagine for a minute the class Saul might have taught there about the transformative work of the Holy Spirit in a believer's life. No opening would be as effective as Saul's personal testimony to God's amazing grace. To underscore the sharp contrast of who he was before he encountered Jesus and who he was now, Saul likely talked about his earlier persecution of Jesus' followers and what motivated him to go after them so furiously. Depending on his listeners, he might even have reflected on the stoning of Stephen that he silently witnessed and, by his presence, tacitly approved.

Most likely Saul's testimony always included his road-to-Damascus encounter with the resurrected Jesus and perhaps Saul's thoughts about the person he had become. Only the Almighty God could have set him on this new path; transformed his heart, mind, and character; and then used this one-time persecutor of Christians to save souls for Jesus. The Holy Spirit undoubtedly used Saul's story to soften listeners' hearts and open them to His transformative power.

Each of us is called to be ready to tell our story, to explain how God helped us move from darkness to truth. Even if the before-Jesus you and the post-conversion you aren't as dramatically different as Saul's before-and-after, your story is still a testimony to the grace of God who helped you see your need for a Savior.

Challenge: Maybe you've spent time writing out your testimony. If not, take some time now: what would you say to a nonbeliever who asked you what makes you different? Then, whether you just now crafted your story or you did so decades ago, choose someone to share it with this week.

DAY 28

A TIME TO MOVE ON

For everything there is a season and a time
for every matter under heaven.
Ecclesiastes 3:1

Saul and Barnabas had been discipling the people in Antioch for a year when, during a time when they as well as the church's prophets and teachers were worshiping the Lord and fasting, the Holy Spirit made known that God was ready for the two to move on: "Set apart for me Barnabas and Saul for the work to which I have called them" (Acts 13:2).

Laying their hands on Saul and Barnabas, the believers in Antioch prayed for the men and sent them off. The Holy Spirit guided them to Seleucia where they boarded a boat to Cyprus, both of them confident that the prophets and teachers they had worshiped with would carry on the important work of discipling and supporting the church in Antioch.

Did you notice as I did how completely void of emotion this account was? I noticed because I remember all too well saying goodbye to the person whom God had sent to disciple me, a new believer at Central Michigan University. On staff with Navigators, Sharla Wolstrom was only at CMU for one year. That was just enough time for her to lead me to Jesus and disciple me. Then she and her husband were on to their next university to disciple others through the ministry of Navigators. My heart was broken when I learned that Sharla would be moving on, but the Holy

Spirit enabled me to send her off with my prayers and my sincere blessings just as the church in Antioch did for Saul and Barnabas.

Challenge: If your beloved pastor or Bible teacher moved on in obedience to the Father, comment on your thoughts, emotions, and faith that all would be well. How long did you wait for God to send you someone else to encourage you in your walk with the Lord? What about this new person made him/her exactly right for that season of your faith journey?

DAY 29

SOWING SEEDS OF TRUTH

*Neither the one who plants nor the one who waters
is anything, but only God who gives the growth.*
1 Corinthians 3:7

Stopping in the city of Salamis on their way to Cyprus, Saul, Barnabas, and John Mark (the author of the gospel of Mark) "proclaimed the word of God in the Jewish synagogues" (Acts 13:5). When they arrived in Paphos, they met a man named Bar-Jesus. This Jewish man was a sorcerer, a magician, a false prophet, and an attendant to Sergius Paulus, the proconsul of Cyprus. Wanting to hear the Word of God, this government leader called for Saul and Barnabas. Hoping to keep the proconsul from coming to faith, Bar-Jesus did not make it easy for the two missionaries—and Paul responded.

Yes, *Paul* responded. Acts 13:9 is the first time in God's Word that Saul (his Hebrew name) is called by his Roman name, Paul. But back to our story.

In the face of Bar-Jesus' opposition, Paul—"filled with the Holy Spirit" (Acts 13:9)—spoke directly to this evil man:

> "You son of the devil, you enemy of all righteousness, full of all deceit and villainy, will you not stop making crooked the straight paths of the Lord? And now listen—the hand of the Lord is against you, and you will be blind for a while." (Acts 13:10–11)

I've wondered why the Holy Spirit made Bar-Jesus blind as opposed to mute or some other disability. Perhaps because Bar-Jesus was already spiritually blind.

More important, though, I am thrilled that Bar-Jesus did not succeed, that Paul and his companions did speak with Sergius Paulus, and that this Roman leader "was astonished at the teaching about the Lord" (Acts 13:12). Paul did his part, and I am sure that the Holy Spirit took it from there.

Challenge: Who sowed seeds of gospel truth in your life when you were spiritually blind? Who in your life today is spiritually blind? What can you learn from the sower in your life about sowing seeds in that person's life? When will you do so?

TINA C. ELACQUA, PH.D.

DAY 30

A BOLD PROCLAMATION

God has brought to Israel a Savior, Jesus.
Acts 13:23

Next stop on the journey of Paul, Barnabas, and John Mark was Perga, where John Mark continued on to Jerusalem, and Barnabas and Paul went to Pisidia Antioch (not the Antioch where believers were first called Christians).

In this Antioch, the Holy Spirit enabled Paul to deliver a powerful message. He eloquently wove together Old Testament prophecy of a Messiah and its fulfillment in Jesus Christ:

> The God of this people Israel chose our ancestors and made the people great during their stay in the land of Egypt, and with uplifted arm he led them out of it.... He gave them their land as an inheritance... he gave them judges... he made David their king.... Of this man's posterity God has brought to Israel a Savior, Jesus. (Acts 13:17, 19–20, 22–23)

In response to this sermon, people asked Paul and Barnabas to teach again the following Sabbath. When they did, "almost the whole city gathered to hear the word of the Lord" (Acts 13:44). Angered by the message, jealous Jewish leaders tried to dispute what Paul had taught—and he wasn't surprised:

"It was necessary that the word of God should be spoken first to you. Since you reject it and judge yourselves to be unworthy of eternal life, we are now turning to the gentiles." (Acts 13:46)

The Jewish leaders then "incited the devout women of high standing and the leading men of the city and stirred up persecution against Paul and Barnabas" (v. 50).

When we take a stand for Jesus—when we choose to flee the world's unrighteous ways and instead to "fight the good fight of the faith" (1 Timothy 6:12), we, too, can expect persecution for letting Jesus Christ shine through us. When we speak gospel truth in our culture today, we can expect persecution for doing the Lord's work. When that happens, we are in the good company of the persecuted Paul.

Challenge: When, if ever, have you responded to God's call to serve only to be rejected? Perhaps you know someone or about someone who has had that experience. Why do you think effective service can result in rejection?

DAY 31

RESPONDING TO PERSECUTION

Rejoice always, pray without ceasing,
give thanks in all circumstances,
for this is the will of God in Christ Jesus for you.
1 Thessalonians 5:16–18

The people of Pisidia Antioch rejected the gospel message and drove the messengers out of town, and as they left, Paul and Barnabas "shook the dust off their feet in protest against them and went to Iconium" (Acts 13:51). How cathartic that action must have been! With that act, these men of God had the last (unspoken) word in this exchange with people who refused the truth.

And Paul and Barnabas were doing just as Jesus Himself had instructed: "If anyone will not welcome you or listen to your words, shake off the dust from your feet as you leave that house or town" (Matthew 10:14). But that was only one aspect of their response to persecution: they were also "filled with joy and with the Holy Spirit" (Acts 13:52).

So how are we to respond when we share the gospel and find our message rejected? Jesus was clear: "Love your enemies, bless those who curse you, do good to those who hate you, and pray for those who spitefully use you and persecute you" (Matthew 5:44 NKJV). Paul himself echoed that instruction—"Bless those who persecute you; bless and do not curse" (Romans 12:14 NKJV)—and he was just getting warmed up. A few verses later, Paul added, "Repay no one evil for evil.... If it is possible, as much as depends on you, live peaceably with all men. Beloved, do not avenge yourselves" (vv. 17–19 NKJV). Reminding believers that vengeance is the Lord's job, Paul was clear: "Do not be overcome by evil, but overcome evil with good" (v. 21 NKJV).

And that's how we are to respond when we are persecuted for Christ's sake.

Challenge: Think about a time when a persecuted believer (maybe you yourself) responded to evil with good. What was the response of the persecutor, the one who had rejected you because of the gospel?

DAY 32

LOVING OUR ENEMIES—AND CONTINUING TO SERVE GOD

I press on toward the goal, toward the prize
of the heavenly call of God in Christ Jesus.
Philippians 3:14

Responding to persecution according to the Bible's instructions doesn't come naturally. Rather than retaliating or exacting revenge, we are to pray for blessings on our enemies, love them, and do good to them. We are to feed them when they're hungry and give them a drink when they're thirsty. As we've also seen, Scripture doesn't ask us to forget or excuse their sin, but to love them with God's love despite their sin. Simply put, we are to overcome evil with good. When we treat our enemies with kindness and the love of Christ, they may repent, turn away from their sin, and even become a friend (see Romans 12:14–21 and 1 Peter 3:1–4).

Leaving vengeance to the Lord, Paul and Barnabas moved on according to the Lord's direction to the city of Iconium in the province of Galatia. Again going to the Jewish synagogue, these men of God—empowered by the Holy Spirit—spoke gospel truth, and "a great number of both Jews and Greeks became believers" (Acts 14:1). Unfortunately, though, not everyone was happy about that. The events in Pisidia Antioch happened here, too: "the unbelieving Jews stirred up the gentiles and poisoned their minds against [Paul and Barnabas]" (v. 2).

Nevertheless, these faithful servants of God "remained for a long time speaking boldly for the Lord, who testified to the word of his grace by granting signs and wonders to be done through them" (Acts 14:3). At some point, though, a group of both Gentiles and Jews tried to stone Paul and Barnabas. Learning of the plot, the two "fled to Lystra and Derbe… and there they continued proclaiming the good news" (vv. 6–7).

Sometimes when persecution hits, God calls us to flee and to then serve in the place God leads you.

Challenge: What can help you respond to your enemies with the love of Christ? And what will enable you to keep serving after you've experienced rejection and even persecution?

DAY 33

KNOWING OUR LORD BETTER

My thoughts are not your thoughts,
*nor are your ways my ways, says the L*ORD.
Isaiah 55:8

We left off with Paul and Barnabas fleeing to Lystra where they "continued proclaiming the good news" (Acts 14:7). At Lystra, Paul also healed a man crippled from birth. The crowds shouted in response, "The gods have come down to us in human form!" (v. 11) and renamed Barnabas, Zeus and Paul, Hermes. Seeing that the people wanted to offer sacrifices to them, Paul and Barnabas tore their clothes, a Jewish act of grief and anguish. Now it was their turn to shout. They told the crowds, "We are mortals just like you" (v. 15).

Then Jews from Antioch and Iconium got involved, riled up the already excited crowd, won them over, and proceeded to stone Paul. At one point, thinking Paul was dead, the people dragged him out of the city. But that was not the end of the story: "When the disciples surrounded him, he got up and went into the city. The next day he went on with Barnabas to Derbe" (Acts 14:20).

Looking back on the persecution he experienced in Antioch, Iconium, and Lystra, Paul referred to these as times the Lord rescued him (see 2 Timothy 3:11). It's easier to see the Lord's rescue in Antioch and Iconium, yet in Lystra He did rescue Paul from death despite the stoning. Clearly, the Lord does not always rescue us the way we want Him to. Instead, the Lord may rescue us in a way that allows us to know Him better and to be drawn into a deeper relationship with Him.

Challenge: Whether it was a rescue, an answer to prayer, an unexpected provision, or a striking demonstration of His protection, comment on a time when God came through for you. Note another time when He came through but not in the way you wanted Him to: what did you learn about God, His character, His ways, or even about yourself that you may not have learned if He had come through the way you wanted Him to?

TINA C. ELACQUA, PH.D.

DAY 34

HARDSHIP REDEEMED

Remain faithful to the Lord with steadfast devotion.
Acts 11:23

Have you noticed that nothing slowed down Paul? Not Bar-Jesus or angry Jewish leaders or fickle townspeople or an attempted stoning! Now in Derbe, Paul—with Barnabas—continued to preach the gospel and make disciples of those who heard and believed the news about Jesus.

But then the Lord led Paul and Barnabas back to the very places where they'd been persecuted, Lystra, Iconium, and Antioch— and Paul understood why. He and Barnabas "strengthened the souls of the disciples and encouraged them to continue in the faith, saying, 'It is through many persecutions that we must enter the kingdom of God'" (Acts 14:22). That message does indeed bring strength and encouragement.

It's freeing to realize that persecution or hardship is inevitable in the Christian's life. Sometimes we endure hardships because of our own sin and disobedience: we say no to the Lord; we choose to do life our way instead of His. But tough times also happen simply because we live with fellow sinners in a fallen world, but God doesn't waste tough times, whatever the cause. Consider the important truth of 1 Peter 1:7:

> These trials will show that your faith is genuine. It is
> being tested as fire tests and purifies gold—though

your faith is far more precious than mere gold. So when your faith remains strong through many trials, it will bring you much praise and glory and honor on the day when Jesus Christ is revealed to the whole world. (NLT)

God can use the hardships we experience to grow our faith in Him. I know that from personal experience, from the trials I have endured in my life. Some resulted from my disobedience, and many came when the Lord allowed someone to exercise free will and do bad things. Whatever the reasons for the hardships, my faith in Jesus Christ has revealed itself as genuine.

Challenge: Whether you realized it was happening in the moment, describe an occasion when hard times resulted in the growth and/or opportunity to live out your faith in Jesus.

DAY 35

TO GOD BE THE GLORY!

The LORD has done great things for us,
and we rejoiced.
Psalm 126:3

Upon their return to Lystra, Iconium, and Antioch (Pisidian) where they had been persecuted, Paul and Barnabas appointed elders to lead the church. Then, with prayer and fasting, "they entrusted [these elders] to the Lord in whom they had come to believe" (Acts 14:23). Paul and Barnabas risked their lives to go back to the very places they had been in danger in order to encourage the saints and to ensure that leadership was in place to carry on the Lord's work.

Then the two men moved on to Pamphylia, spoke God's Word in Perga, and continued to Attalia. From there, they sailed back to Antioch of Syria, where Paul and Barnabas had founded the Gentile Christian church and where they'd been sent out as missionaries. Their first missionary journey was now complete, and they had stories to tell about how God had blessed their evangelistic and discipleship efforts. Calling together the church, Paul and Barnabas "related all that God had done with them and how he had opened a door of faith for the gentiles" (Acts 14:27).

Do you do that? Do you make a point of sharing all that God has done for you? Doing so gives God glory and you, a more thankful heart. Telling what God has done for you also keeps you both more expectant and aware of Jesus' ongoing work in your life and of His continuing blessings of guidance, provision, protection, and presence with you. Follow the example that Paul and Barnabas offer us and tell others specifically how good God has been to you—and I encourage you to do so daily.

Challenge: A good way to develop the habit of telling others how God is working in your life—and the habit of thanking Him—is to keep a record. The discipline of writing down the ways God has guided you, provided for you, and answered your prayers will fuel your gratitude and keep at the forefront of your mind stories of His goodness that you can tell when the opportunity arises.

TINA C. ELACQUA, PH.D.

DAY 36

A DISAGREEMENT— REDEEMED!

Barnabas wanted to take with them John called Mark. But Paul decided not to take with them one who had deserted them in Pamphylia.
Acts 15:37–38

Paul and Barnabas had been a dynamic duo when they traveled together on Paul's first missionary journey. One key moment in their partnership occurred in Jerusalem when they participated in a discussion of circumcision with the apostles and elders there. Peter, the apostle whom God had called to share the gospel with Gentiles, pointed out that these believers had been given the Holy Spirit just as Jewish believers had. Peter also reiterated that people are saved by grace, not by anything we do, and that meant not by being circumcised.

In support of Peter's assertion, Paul and Barnabas "told of all the signs and wonders that God had done through them among the gentiles" (Acts 15:12), Then James spoke up: "I have reached the decision that we should not trouble those gentiles who are turning to God" (v. 19). Accompanied by Judas and Silas, Paul and Barnabas headed to Antioch with news of this decision.

After a few days in Antioch, Paul proposed to Barnabas retracing their steps and visiting again those cities where they had preached the gospel. Barnabas was open to the idea, and he wanted to take along John Mark, his cousin. Feeling that John Mark had deserted him in Pamphylia, Paul did not want him along on this trip. When the disagreement grew too intense, Barnabas and John Mark sailed away to Cyprus. Paul chose Silas to accompany him, and the two set out for Syria and Cilicia to strengthen the churches there (Acts 15:36–41).

Interesting that this disagreement resulted in two mission trips, not just one. The Lord works in mysterious ways, doesn't He?

Challenge: When, if ever, have you seen or heard about a ministry increasing in effectiveness and/or reach as a result of a disagreement or other unfortunate event? Share details about how God redeemed what seemed like a disaster and advanced His kingdom work.

DAY 37

LESSONS FROM PAUL
AND TIMOTHY

*Don't let anyone think less of you
because you are young.*
1 Timothy 4:12 (NLT)

Upon leaving Antioch, Paul and Silas traveled on to Derbe and
then to Lystra where they met a young man named Timothy.
The son of a Jewish mother who believed in Jesus and a Greek
father, Timothy was "well spoken of by the brothers and sisters
in Lystra and Iconium" (Acts 16:2). Clearly Timothy's fellow
believers recognized what Paul did. In a future letter to Timothy,
the apostle would commend him for his "sincere faith, a faith that
lived first in your grandmother Lois and your mother Eunice and
now, I am sure, lives in you" (2 Timothy 1:5). But back to their
first meeting in Lystra, Timothy's youth did not deter Paul from
having him travel and serve the Lord with him.

As the two men went from town to town, "the churches
were strengthened in the faith and increased in numbers daily"
(Acts 16:5). Of course traveling with Paul meant learning from
the apostle, and this mentoring role led to Timothy eventually
pastoring the church at Ephesus (1 Timothy 1:3) and being a
valued and respected co-worker. Paul, for instance, began his letter
to the Philippians with "Paul and Timothy, servants of Christ
Jesus" (1:1). Paul had chosen young Timothy to join him in God's
work and then invested in his spiritual growth, setting an example

of the invaluable mentoring a long-time believer can offer someone younger in the faith.

Whatever their age, if people are believers, they have Jesus' Holy Spirit living in them. His presence equips them for service. Age simply does not matter. God can and does use all His children, whatever our age, in His kingdom work.

Challenge: When have you been especially touched, inspired, or encouraged by a young person's faith in God? And here's a topic for prayer: whom might God want you to mentor or be mentored by?

DAY 38

UNEQUALLY YOKED

Do not be mismatched with unbelievers.
2 Corinthians 6:14

In Acts 16:1 we met "a disciple named Timothy, the son of a Jewish woman who was a believer, but his father was a Greek." That word *but* acknowledges the less-than-ideal marriage between a Jew and a Greek. In 2 Corinthians 6, Paul stated the principle and then asked rhetorical questions to make his point:

> How can righteousness be a partner with wickedness? How can light live with darkness? What harmony can there be between Christ and the devil? How can a believer be a partner with an unbeliever? And what union can there be between God's temple and idols? For we [believers] are the temple of the living God. (vv. 14–16 NLT)

All of God's commands are for our well-being, and here He warned us believers to not lock ourselves into binding relationships, business or personal, with unbelievers. Doing so could weaken our commitment to Jesus and impair our efforts to live with integrity and according to God's standards.

"Don't be unequally yoked," though, is a difficult rule to follow when, for instance, we long for a child, but the prospect of a Christian husband is slim, if it even exists at all. Each of us struggles to trust our most cherished dreams and hopes to God and His timing, but choosing to trust Him is the wisest way.

If you're already yoked to an unbeliever, I encourage you to be in prayer, asking the Lord to graciously bring your spouse to faith. If you have children, be encouraged by Timothy: with one believing parent, he became a follower of Jesus.

Trust the Lord to bring good to a mismatch, whether in your personal or your business life, for His glory and purposes. Nothing is impossible for the Lord!

Challenge: What day-to-day aspects of life are more difficult when a married couple is unequally yoked? In what specific ways can that yoke impact a person's walk with Jesus? If you're single, keep in mind these challenges. If you're married to an unbeliever, ask God to bring good from the marriage.

TINA C. ELACQUA, PH.D.

DAY 39

GOD'S GUIDANCE

Make me to know your ways, O Lord;
teach me your paths.
Psalm 25:4

The missionary journeys in Acts are fascinating for many reasons, but I especially appreciate the example they offer of how God guides us in life.

Acts 16:6, for instance, tells us that Paul and his companions "went through the region of Phrygia and Galatia, having been forbidden by the Holy Spirit to speak the word in Asia." We then read that "the Spirit of Jesus did not allow them to go into Bithynia" (v. 7). So Paul and his traveling companions went to Troas. That night Paul was told in a vision to go to Macedonia. In what ways does God speak to us today?

God speaks to us today through the Holy Spirit who lives in believers. God also speaks to us through the Bible, prayer, circumstances, and the church. He guides us by aligning these five areas. He did so for me, for example, when I sought a certain faculty post.

During prayer I sensed the Spirit telling me to apply for the position. The Lord even gave me Scripture confirming that idea. As for the circumstances, all my colleagues agreed I would be a good choice for the position. My church at the time and fellow believers all saw the position as a great fit and believed God was directing me to it. When the position was offered, I confidently accepted it. Then, at the orientation, the administrator opened with a devotional using the same Scripture God had given me in my prayer time. God's sources of guidance had truly aligned!

When the Holy Spirit told Paul and his companions to not go into Asia at that time, God may have guided Paul in many of these same ways.

Challenge: God guides our path through the Holy Spirit, the Bible, prayer, circumstances, and the church. Which of these do you tend not to consult? Which do you tend to dismiss? Tell of a time when the five aligned and God clearly guided you.

DAY 40

GOING WHERE GOD LED

"Here on earth you will have many trials and sorrows."
Jesus in John 16:33 (NLT)

When Paul had a vision of a man in Macedonia saying, "Come over to Macedonia and help us" (Acts 16:9), Paul, Silas, Timothy, and Dr. Luke, the author of the book of Acts, obeyed immediately. These men of faith were "convinced that God had called [them] to proclaim the good news" there (v. 10). When they stopped in Philippi on the way to Macedonia, Paul met Lydia, a seller of expensive purple cloth. When Lydia heard the truth about Jesus that Paul preached, she believed and became the first European Christian. She as well as members of her household were baptized, proclaiming publicly the inner change of heart from sinner to saint that had happened when they named Jesus Christ as their Lord.

One day, as Paul and his companions were going to the place of prayer, they encountered a demon-possessed slave girl, a fortune-teller who earned a lot of money for her masters. She followed Paul and his crew shouting, "These men are slaves of the Most High God, who proclaim to you the way of salvation" (Acts 16:17). After she had done this for many days, a very annoyed Paul turned and said to the demon, "I order you in the name of Jesus Christ to come out of her" (v. 18), and instantly the demon left her. Seeing their income source dried up, her enraged masters dragged Paul and Silas before city authorities. Hearing the crowd's accusations of the two men, the officials ordered them stripped, beaten with wooden rods, and thrown into prison with their feet placed in stocks.

Challenge: In light of these two snapshots from Paul and Silas's missionary journey, what conclusion can you draw about God's guidance? Hint: Does He always call us to sunshine and butterflies? Explain the benefits of understanding and remembering this truth.

TINA C. ELACQUA, PH.D.

DAY 41

PRAISE, AN EARTHQUAKE, AND SALVATION

In your righteousness deliver me and rescue me.
Psalm 71:2

Stripped, beaten, thrown into prison, put in stocks—this is where Paul and Silas found themselves as a result of delivering a girl from a demon and thereby depriving her masters of their income source. Imagine the humiliation, the physical pain, the hunger they're feeling, perhaps some frustration at the turn of events, maybe some puzzlement about what's next—all this as they sat in the dark prison cell with its stagnant air and rough wooden stocks that kept them in the same position for hours.

Yet Paul and Silas responded by "praying and singing hymns to God" (Acts 16:25). Suddenly a massive earthquake shook the prison, making doors fly open and the prisoners' chains fall off. The jailer woke up to see the prison doors wide open. Assuming the prisoners had escaped and knowing that would cost him his life, he drew his sword to kill himself. But Paul shouted, "Do not harm yourself, for we are all here!" (v. 28). The jailer fell down before these two unusual prisoners and asked the most important question ever: "What must I do to be saved?" (v. 30). Paul and Silas replied, "Believe in the Lord Jesus, and you will be saved" (v. 31).

Then Paul and Silas shared this message with everyone in the jailer's household. After he washed the men's wounds, the jailer and his family were baptized. He then welcomed Paul and Silas into his house and fed them, "and he and his entire household rejoiced that he had become a believer in God" (Acts 16:34).

Imprisonment, praise, an earthquake, salvation—what an unexpected yet God-ordained turn of events!

Challenge: Now, in light of how Paul and Silas's experience unfolded, what conclusion can you draw about God's guidance? Put differently, how might you refine your conclusion from the preceding day's devotional? What impact does this unexpected chain of events have on your understanding of God's guidance?

DAY 42

SONGS FROM PRISON

I will always sing praises to your name.
Psalm 61:8

Following God does not mean being protected from all heartache and pain. We've seen God allow Paul and Silas, two men on fire for the Lord, to be flogged and imprisoned. We can be encouraged, though, to see how God used their pain for His glory and purposes. The jailer who had heard the prisoners singing praise despite their circumstances also heard the gospel and believed—as did everyone in his household (see Acts 16:16–34).

Let's think for a minute about prison and whether you yourself have ever been in a prison. I haven't been in a prison made of steel bars, but I have felt imprisoned by tragedy and grief. During my darkest hours, I questioned God, His nature, and His goodness. I doubted that He actually had a good plan for my life. I wouldn't be surprised if Paul and Silas had similar thoughts. Having proclaimed that Jesus is Lord, as God had called them to do, Paul and Silas found themselves in prison. Yet during their darkest hours there, Paul and Silas sang hymns to the Lord.

That response to pain is not natural or impossible. I have stood in church singing praise songs to the Lord as tears streamed down my face. I have chosen—as Paul and Silas did—to sing of God's goodness and love when pain threatened to suffocate me. And you know what happened? Just as Paul and Silas were set free from their physical prison, in time, I, too, have been set free from my pain and my doubts.

Friends, sing out to the Lord even in your darkest hours.

Challenge: What pain in your life has provided an opportunity for someone to hear the gospel message of Jesus and be saved? And when, if ever, have you chosen to sing praise despite the severe pain you were experiencing? What resulted from that choice? Maybe now is the time for you to discover how God meets you when you praise Him in darkness.

DAY 43

BEING A VIGILANT STUDENT OF GOD'S WORD

Whatever was written in former days
was written for our instruction.
Romans 15:4

Next stop on Paul's second missionary journey was the city of Thessalonica, about 100 miles from Philippi. As was his practice, Paul went first to the Jewish synagogue. Knowing that the Jews were familiar with the Old Testament, Paul began "explaining and proving that it was necessary for the Messiah to suffer and to rise from the dead" (Acts 17:3). Some Jews, a great many of the devout Greeks, and many women recognized and embraced Paul's teaching as the truth.

Very aware of this response, the Jews were jealous: "with the help of some ruffians in the marketplaces they formed a mob and set the city in an uproar" (Acts 17:5). For the safety of Paul and Silas, the new believers in Thessalonica sent them off to Berea, and as was their habit, the two men went to the synagogue there. These synagogue Jews were more receptive than the ones in Thessalonica had been. In fact—setting an important example for you and me—they didn't merely listen to the gospel message. Every day they examined the Scriptures to confirm that this itinerant teacher's message completely aligned with God's Word. Acknowledging the truth of Paul's words, "Many of them therefore believed, including not a few Greek women and men of high standing" (Acts 17:12).

When the Jews of Thessalonica heard of Paul's success in Berea, though, they traveled the 50 miles on foot to stir up the people of Berea against the apostle just as they had done in Thessalonica.

Undoubtedly shaking his head over the jealous Jews of Thessalonica, our sovereign God moved Paul on to Athens.

Challenge: When you hear a message taught or preached, do you open God's Word to confirm its accuracy? We would do well to follow the example of the Bereans and always see if a message we hear lines up with God's Word.

TINA C. ELACQUA, PH.D.

DAY 44

IDOLATRY THEN AND NOW

"You shall have no other gods before me."
God in Exodus 20:3

With his second journey seemingly guided by protests in Thessalonica and Berea, Paul found himself in Athens where he was "deeply distressed" by the abundance of idols in the city (Acts 17:16). Everywhere he looked as he walked around, Paul saw objects of worship, including an altar dedicated "To an unknown god" (v. 23).

As the center of Greek culture, philosophy, and education, Athens was home to a large number of philosophers and educated men who were always willing to hear and debate new ideas and different ways of thinking. So they didn't hesitate to invite the newcomer to speak, and Paul began with a reference to their unknown god. He then moved easily into a discussion of the God they didn't know but whom he knew: the one true God of the Hebrew Scriptures, the Creator of the world, the Giver of life, and the Lord of all. This one true God is not a deity that can be represented in gold, silver, or stone. This one true God wants people to seek after Him, find Him, and live in the freedom of forgiveness and the joy of relationship with Him:

> While God has overlooked the times of human ignorance, now he commands all people everywhere to repent. (Acts 17:30)

Judgment will come, Paul warned. Then his vague closing reference to resurrection from the dead made some in the audience scoff, some listeners wanted to hear more, and still others believed.

Today people still scoff.

Challenge: Consider for a moment the idols in our culture and even in your own life. What are people pursuing in hopes of fulfillment, significance, or purpose? What cause, person, or goal has taken the preeminent place of God for some people? Now, closer to home, what in your life tends to push God aside? What competes for your attention and devotion—and what can you do to keep God on the throne of your life? Be specific and practical—and then just do it!

DAY 45

CHRISTIAN COMMUNITY IS KEY

*You are the body of Christ, and
each one of you is a part of it.*
1 Corinthians 12:27 (NIV)

Paul's attempt to introduce the Athenian philosophers and deep thinkers to the one true God was met with scoffers as well as people who wanted to hear more. Yet the next verse says simply, "At that point Paul left them" (Acts 17:33) with no reference to an intervening amount of time or to whether he was persecuted or pressured in some other way to leave. Two verses later we read that Paul had gone to Corinth.

As Paul waited for Timothy and Silas to arrive from Athens, God blessed him with a connection to fellow believers: a Jewish man named Aquila and his wife, Priscilla, who were tentmakers just as Paul was. Once again God did not leave Paul to work or live alone: "he stayed with [Aquila and Priscilla], and they worked together.... Every Sabbath he would argue in the synagogue and would try to convince Jews and Greeks" (Acts 18:3–4).

In fact, when Timothy and Silas arrived in Corinth, they found Paul "proclaiming the word, testifying to the Jews that the Messiah was Jesus" (Acts 18:5). As had happened before, Paul's listeners rejected the message, so he "shook the dust from his clothes," announced he would now take the message to the gentiles, and left the synagogue (v. 6). In His sovereign plan, God used the Jews' rejection of the gospel message to give Gentiles the opportunity to receive salvation.

Challenge: God never had Paul do life or his ministry work alone. Are you choosing to walk the Christian life alone? Why or why not? If you are flying solo, what dangers might you face? (See, for instance, Ecclesiastes 4:9–12; Proverbs 11:14, 15:22, 18:1; and 1 Peter 5:8.) If you've chosen to be part of a Christian community, what blessings have come with that? Doing life alone is not God's way. Walking intimately with Christ, surrounded with others who are like-minded, is God's plan for us.

DAY 46

PROCLAIM THE GOSPEL MESSAGE!

I solemnly urge you: proclaim the message; be persistent whether the time is favorable or unfavorable; convince, rebuke, and encourage with the utmost patience in teaching.
2 Timothy 4:1–2

While Paul was in Corinth, the Lord gave him an important message of encouragement through a vision:

> "Do not be afraid, but speak and do not be silent, for I am with you, and no one will lay a hand on you to harm you, for there are many in this city who are my people." (Acts 18:9–10)

What an incredible blessing! The Lord Almighty Himself told Paul to not hold back the truth, to not be quiet about the gospel, to preach boldly, and to do so without fear because God was with him.

That promise is for you and me too. First, though, it challenges us to consider where and with whom we are holding back and not letting others see the light of Jesus Christ in us or hear us speak the gospel message. Jesus Himself spoke this hard truth: "Whoever denies me before others, I also will deny before my Father in heaven" (Matthew 10:33). May this statement be a wake-up call, prompting us to share the gospel boldly, confident that God is with us.

Again, the words of encouragement to preach boldly are God's words to us just as they were to Paul. God also told Paul that many people, even within the wicked city of Corinth, already belonged to Him. Surely God would continue to bring people to a saving knowledge of Jesus as Paul preached the gospel truth.

Paul stayed in Corinth for a year and a half, faithfully teaching the gospel message. He spoke boldly, trusting God's presence, protection, and favor.

Challenge: Is God's message to Paul also a message for you? In what ways, if any, are you holding back and not letting others see the light of Jesus Christ in you or hear you speak the gospel message? Are you worried you may be scoffed at, ridiculed, or rejected? Talk to God about this. Ask Him to work in your heart.

DAY 47

THE BATTLE AND THE ARMOR

Be strong in the Lord and in the strength of his power.
Ephesians 6:10

After staying in Corinth, Paul set sail for Syria with the goal of returning to Antioch. But first we read, "At Cenchreae he had his hair cut, for he was under a vow" (Acts 18:18). Let me explain.

Numbers 6 describes the Nazirite vow. When men or women desired to devote themselves exclusively to the Lord, they made a vow to Him. Deciding voluntarily to set themselves apart for the Lord, they didn't cut their hair or beard, drink wine or strong drink, or touch a dead body. Humbly acknowledging his need for the Lord's help to stand strong against evil and temptation, Paul made this vow that would help him stay focused on the Lord.

Like Paul in his "good fight of the faith" (1 Timothy 6:12), we need the Lord's help to stand strong against evil and temptation, and a vow of renewed devotion to God could serve us well. We can, for instance, commit to praying God's Word, meditating on and memorizing Scripture, getting godly counsel, having a prayer and accountability partner, and more fully surrendering our heart and mind to God's ways. Also, the Lord has provided His armor for us because—as Paul explained—we are battling against "the spiritual forces of evil in the heavenly places" (Ephesians 6:12).

To help us stand strong, the Lord has provided us with the belt of truth, the breastplate of righteousness, shoes of peace to wear as we proclaim the gospel of Jesus Christ, the shield of faith, the helmet of salvation, and the sword of the Spirit, a reference to God's Word (see Ephesians 6:10–18). Not knowing what a day will hold, we would do well to put on our armor every morning.

Challenge: Share your thoughts about what it means to put on the armor of God. How do you go about—or how would you like to go about it? Consider, too, the strength available to you during the times you spend with God, as you live out your commitment to Scripture and prayer, and in your relationships with fellow believers.

DAY 48

SHARING THE GOSPEL

*How are they to believe in him of
whom they have never heard?*
Romans 10:14 (ESV)

When Paul left Corinth and sailed for Syria, Priscilla and Aquila joined him. Their first stop was the port of Ephesus, a main city in Asia and an important trading route. Aware of the large Jewish population in Ephesus, Paul went to the synagogue. Even though he didn't plan on staying in the city long, Paul didn't pass on the opportunity to plant seeds of gospel truth. He was soon on his way, sailing from Ephesus to the port of Caesarea. He visited the church at Jerusalem before heading to Antioch of Syria, the very church that originally commissioned him. This stop marked the end of Paul's second missionary journey.

After an unspecified amount of time in Antioch, Paul began his third missionary journey, traveling throughout Galatia and Phrygia. Having previously preached the gospel there, Paul now wanted to encourage the believers.

Arriving in Ephesus, Paul met a dozen or so followers of John the Baptist who had believed his message and been baptized. When Paul explained that John had been pointing to Jesus, the people believed, Paul baptized them, and the Holy Spirit descended as He had at Pentecost, enabling these believers to prophesy and speak in tongues.

Paul also went to the synagogue where "for three months [he] spoke out boldly and argued persuasively about the kingdom of God" (Acts 19:8). When some refused to believe, Paul changed venues and began teaching daily in the lecture hall of Tyrannus. The fruit of Paul's two years of teaching at Tyrannus was remarkable: "all the residents of Asia, both Jews and Greeks, heard the word of the Lord" (v. 10). Paul obeyed, and God blessed.

Challenge: Wherever God directed, Paul preached the gospel. Ask God to show you who in your world needs to hear the truth about Jesus Christ. Then in a step of obedience and faith, grab coffee with one of those people. A good starting point is talking about your relationship with Jesus and the difference He's made in your life.

TINA C. ELACQUA, PH.D.

DAY 49

GOD'S TAILORED APPROACH

Set your mind and heart to seek the Lord your God.
1 Chronicles 22:19

We've seen how God blessed Paul's bold preaching, but sometimes He empowered Paul in a different way. We read in Acts 19, for instance, that "God did extraordinary miracles through Paul" (v. 11). God chose to do this in Ephesus, a place of wizards, sorcerers, witches, astrologers, fortune-tellers, and magical incantations. Like today, people were interested in the supernatural and the unseen world. As a result, people ended up pursuing Satan instead of Jesus.

No wonder Deuteronomy 18:10–11 says, "Do not... practice fortune-telling, or use sorcery, or interpret omens, or engage in witchcraft, or cast spells, or function as mediums or psychics, or call forth the spirits of the dead" (NLT). Satan is the power behind these occult practices just as he is behind horoscopes, fortune-telling, palm reading, tarot cards, witchcraft, and cults today. (A brief aside: better than knowing the future is knowing personally the sovereign God who reigns over the future as well as the present. Don't turn to Satan, the deceiver. Turn instead to the one true God through a relationship with Jesus Christ.)

Back in Ephesus, God did this miracle: "when the handkerchiefs or aprons that had touched [Paul's] skin were brought to the sick, their diseases left them, and the evil spirits came out of them" (Acts 19:12).

God knew that Paul would not let the nonbelievers in Ephesus think he was a magician or that the apparent healing power of the handkerchiefs and aprons was the result of some hocus-pocus or trickery. And Paul knew that God intended the remarkable healings to turn the eyes of the people to Him.

Challenge: In what ways was God's choice to do an extraordinary miracle in Ephesus fitting for that city? In what way(s) tailored perfectly for you did God meet you and lead you to accept Jesus as your Savior or Lord? Then tell of a specific and very personal way God made His presence with you obvious in just the past week. Thank Him for His personal love.

DAY 50

CLEANING HOUSE

Submit yourselves therefore to God. Resist the devil, and he will flee from you. Draw near to God, and he will draw near to you. Cleanse your hands... and purify your hearts.
James 4:7–8

Not only did the people whom God had healed or freed from the grasp of evil spirits recognize His power, Jewish exorcists who made a living by going from town to town claiming to heal and cast out demons also noticed the undeniable power—and wanted it. They thought that simply including the name of Jesus in their command to an evil spirit would bring success: "I command you in the name of Jesus, whom Paul preaches, to come out!" (Acts 19:13 NLT).

Hearing those words from one of those exorcists, the evil spirit replied with "Jesus I know, and Paul I know, but who are you?" (Acts 19:15). Then the man in whom the evil spirit resided attacked the Jewish exorcists so violently that they ran away naked and battered.

This news traveled fast all through Ephesus. Jews and Greeks alike found a new respect for Jesus, "and the name of the Lord Jesus was praised" (Acts 19:17). In a striking demonstration that they recognized Jesus' power, some of the city's magicians gathered their incantation books—valued at several million of today's dollars—and burned them at a public bonfire. At great personal cost, these people ended their participation in practices that did not please God.

Like those magicians who burned their books, may we let nothing hinder our relationship with Jesus. That goal probably means we need to do some housecleaning.

Challenge: What do you, figuratively speaking, need to gather and burn? Are certain shows, movies, books, or magazines not in line with God's best for you? If you're not sure, simply ask the Lord to show you: "Search me, O God, and know my heart; test me and know my thoughts. See if there is any wicked way in me, and lead me in the way everlasting" (Psalm 139:23–24). Get rid of whatever God reveals to you.

DAY 51

DEAFENED BY DOLLARS

"You cannot serve God and wealth."
Jesus in Matthew 6:24

Sometimes economics explains a lot. In Acts 19, for instance, Paul's preaching was drawing people toward Jesus and away from their worship at the shrines to Artemis. Those shrines, however, were great sources of income for the silversmiths of Ephesus, and these craftsmen were very concerned about this threat to their livelihood.

As a silversmith who made shrines to this false god of fertility, Demetrius addressed the situation in hopes of stirring up a riot:

> In almost the whole of Asia this Paul has persuaded and drawn away a considerable number of people by saying that gods made with hands are not gods. And there is danger not only that this trade of ours may come into disrepute but also that the temple of the great goddess Artemis will be scorned, and she will be deprived of her majesty that brought all Asia and the world to worship her." (Acts 19:26–27)

Infuriated by these words, the crowd seized two of Paul's traveling companions and ran to the theater. Paul wanted to address the mob there, but the disciples and even some government officials urged him not to. When Alexander, a Jewish man, tried to defend the truth of Paul's message, the crowd responded with two hours of yelling, "Great is Artemis of the Ephesians!" (Acts 19:28). Finally, the town clerk settled the crowd, reasoned with them, and dismissed the assembly.

Challenge: The silversmiths of Ephesus were deaf to the gospel truth Paul was preaching. They couldn't afford to hear and believe: the cost was their livelihood, and that cost was too high. Even if you're already a follower of Jesus, what, if anything, interferes with your ability to hear and/or respond to God's truth? Which of the world's priorities tempt you to stray from the Lord? What will you do to stand strong against those influences?

DAY 52

RESURRECTION

"I am the resurrection and the life. Those who believe in me, even though they die, will live, and everyone who lives and believes in me will never die."
Jesus in John 11:25–26

Clearly, it was none too soon for Paul to get out of Ephesus. He offered his disciples encouragement for their kingdom work and said farewell. He headed to Macedonia, went to Greece for three months, and was about to go to Syria when he learned of a plot against him. So he headed for Troas.

The night before he was planning to leave Troas, Paul wanted to take full advantage of his time with these believers, so he was still teaching at midnight. All had gathered in an upstairs room (remember, heat rises!), and many lamps were lit, offering a peaceful flickering light. And the hour got later and later. One person in the room—his name was Eutychus, and he was probably between eight and fourteen years old—had perched on a windowsill. "While Paul talked still longer" (Acts 20:9), Eutychus sank off into a deep sleep... fell out the window, down three floors, and died.

Paul immediately stopped talking and went down to Eutychus. Lifting him up, Paul said to the people around him, "Do not be alarmed, for his life is in him" (Acts 20:10).

Having rejoined Paul's missionary team, Dr. Luke was present at this marathon teaching, and we can certainly trust his confirmation of both the death and the revival of Eutychus. God healed this young boy, and God is still in the business of raising people from the dead, spiritually, physically, and eternally. Spiritual resurrection is marked by salvation; a believer's physical resurrection will happen when Jesus returns; and we will live with Him forever!

Challenge: What does it mean to be dead in one's sin? When you experienced life after that death—when you named Jesus your Savior—what was one of the most striking contrasts between the dead-in-your-sins you and the you in your new life? Also, what difference in a believer's life does the hope of heaven—the truth that believers will live forever with Jesus—make or could it make?

DAY 53

READY TO DIE FOR JESUS

I do not count my life of any value to myself,
if only I may finish my course and the ministry that I
received from the Lord Jesus, to testify to
the good news of God's grace.
Acts 20:24

Look again at that Acts 20:24 statement of Paul. It was part of his heartfelt words of farewell to his beloved church in Ephesus. Heading to Jerusalem, Paul knew he might not see them again. After all, Paul explained, "The Holy Spirit testifies to me in every city that imprisonment and persecutions are waiting for me" (v. 23).

After Paul shared words of affirmation and encouragement, he and the leaders of the Ephesian church prayed together. Then, Luke reported, "There was much weeping among them all; they embraced Paul and kissed him, grieving especially because of what he had said, that they would not see him again" (Acts 20:37–38).

As he traveled, Paul kept ministering to fellow believers. Even on a seven-day stay in the Syrian port of Tyre, he "looked up the disciples" to encourage them in their faith (Acts 21:4). He did the same in the city of Ptolemais, and then he visited Philip the evangelist. While he was at Philip's, a prophet named Agabus came from Judea with a message for Paul. Taking the apostle's belt, Agabus tied his own hands and feet with it. Then he explained: "Thus says the Holy Spirit, 'This is the way the Jews in Jerusalem will bind the man who owns this belt and will hand him over to the gentiles'" (v. 11).

Just as the disciples in Tyre had done, these believers begged Paul not to go into Jerusalem. To this Paul replied, "What are you doing, weeping and breaking my heart? For I am ready not only to be bound but even to die in Jerusalem for the name of the Lord Jesus" (Acts 21:13).

Challenge: Comment on Paul's faith and his unwavering commitment to the Lord. Why is he able to stand strong? What about his example can you apply to your own life of faith?

DAY 54

THREE ASPECTS OF FAITH

Fight the good fight of the faith.
1 Timothy 6:12

Despite the warning that he would be bound and handed over to the Gentiles (Acts 21:11), Paul headed to Jerusalem. His commitment to Jesus would not be weakened by a mere threat of death!

After being greeted warmly by the brothers in Christ, Paul and his companions visited Jesus' brother James and heard about the thousands of Jewish believers and their zeal for the law that had unfortunately resulted in a misunderstanding. These believers thought Paul was teaching Jewish Christians living among Gentiles to not circumcise their children. But Paul had actually told those Jewish believers not to insist that Gentile Christians circumcise their children. The reason is simple: circumcision has nothing to do with salvation. In Paul's day and even today, Christians can be sidetracked by nonessentials of the faith, by those practices and traditions that are not critical to salvation.

After Paul had been in Jerusalem for almost a week, the Jews from Asia stirred up the whole crowd. A mob seized Paul and tried to kill him. Hearing the uproar and wanting to avoid a riot, the Roman commander arrested Paul, ordering his soldiers to carry Paul on their shoulders to protect him from the violent mob. As people yelled, "Kill him, kill him!" (Acts 21:36 NLT), Paul asked the commander if he could speak to the people. Granted permission, Paul motioned for silence and, addressing the people in their own language, Aramaic, he shared his testimony.

Challenge: In this action-packed section of Scripture, we see three aspects of faith. Which one is most relevant to you today—and how will you respond?

- What nonessentials of the Christian faith are sidetracking you?
- What opportunity do you have to go above and beyond to reconcile a misunderstanding especially when the confusion involves a fellow believer?
- What can you do to prepare to be bolder than comes naturally the next time you have an occasion to share your testimony?

The Lord will help you with the aspect of your faith that you choose.

DAY 55

ONE GOSPEL, ONE BODY

We were all baptized into one body—
Jews or Greeks, slaves or free.
1 Corinthians 12:13

When we last saw our hero, Paul was sharing his testimony with a crowd in Jerusalem—and what a testimony it was! In a very remarkable way, God had gotten the attention of this murderer of Christians and then transformed him into a committed follower of Jesus and preacher to the Gentiles. And how did the riled-up people respond? Surely not in the way Paul had hoped.

The crowd shouted, "Away with such a fellow from the earth! For he should not be allowed to live" (Acts 22:22). This outcry for his death was hardly the outcome Paul had prayed for and desired. His bold testimony to a hostile crowd did not result in the success of conversions, but his proclamation of Jesus' impact on his life was a different kind of success: Paul had obeyed Jesus' calling on his life. Paul had sown seeds of truth. Now the Holy Spirit could do His job: convict people of their sin and help them recognize Jesus as their Savior and the Messiah. And back to our story....

At the crowd's outburst, the Roman commander took Paul inside the army barracks and, hoping to "find out the reason for this outcry against him," ordered him "to be examined by flogging" (Acts 22:24). After the soldiers tied him up, Paul asked the simple question "Is it legal for you to flog a Roman person who is uncondemned?" (v. 25). This naturally born citizen of Rome should not have been bound and should not be flogged.

Challenge: Paul shared his testimony with the very mob that tried to kill him. They had quieted down and even seemed to listen as he told them about Jesus. Why do you think the people shouted for Paul's death when he said that God had sent him to share the gospel with the Gentiles (Acts 22:21)? If you're feeling that certain people shouldn't hear or don't deserve to hear the gospel, ask God for the necessary heart change.

DAY 56

GOD'S INTERVENTION

God is our refuge and strength,
a very present help in trouble.
Psalm 46:1

Still curious about why the Jews were so against Paul, the next day the commander released Paul to allow him to speak before the chief priests and entire council. Their reception of Paul was no more gracious or accepting than the crowd of Jews the day before. Their response is described with words like *dissension, division, a great clamor,* and *violence* (Acts 23:7, 9–10).

Again God used the Roman commander to save Paul. Afraid some people who had heard Paul speak "would tear Paul to pieces" (Acts 23:10), the commander ordered his soldiers to rescue the apostle and take him back to the army barracks. Well aware of His faithful servant's frame of mind, "that night the Lord stood near him and said, 'Keep up your courage! For just as you have testified for me in Jerusalem, so you must bear witness also in Rome'" (v. 11).

But the peace Paul undoubtedly knew with the Lord's words was not to last. The next morning more than 40 Jews made an oath to not eat or drink anything until they had killed Paul. These conspirators even asked the chief priests to call Paul before the council so they could kill him on his way. The Lord intervened and saved Paul's life once again: Paul's nephew heard of this plan, told Paul, and then, at Paul's direction, told the Roman commander.

The Lord used this unbeliever to move Paul out of Jerusalem to Caesarea, thereby enabling him to avoid the ambush. And what a sight that must have been! Two hundred soldiers, 70 horsemen, and 200 spearmen escorted Paul safely out of Jerusalem.

Challenge: I love how God uses nonbelievers as well as believers to do His work. When has He used a nonbeliever in your life? Be specific. I also love that God meets us when we're discouraged. If that's you right now, know that God is aware. Expect Him to offer encouragement—whether directly to you, through His people, or in His written Word.

TINA C. ELACQUA, PH.D.

DAY 57

OUR DELIVERER

This poor soul cried and was heard by the LORD
and was saved from every trouble.
Psalm 34:6

The 200 soldiers, 70 horsemen, and 200 spearmen were quite the procession to Caesarea where they safely delivered Paul to Felix, the governor of Judea. Sometimes God works in big ways! Earlier in Acts, we read that while the guards slept on either side of Peter, an angel walked him out of prison (see Acts 12). When Paul and Silas were in a prison cell, God sent an earthquake that shook the building's foundation, broke the prisoners' chains, and opened the cell doors (see Acts 16). Now, again acting in a big way and providing an escort of almost 500 people, God delivered Paul from a murderous plot.

Paul arrived with a letter for Felix from the Roman commander. He explained that he and his soldiers had rescued Paul from some Jews who were about to kill him and that he'd allowed Paul to speak to the high council in hopes of learning the basis for the crowd's accusations. The Roman commander rightly told the governor that the charges against Paul were due to religious law and that Paul was certainly not guilty of anything deserving imprisonment or death. Having learned of a plot to kill him, the commander thought it best to send Paul as well as his accusers to the governor for a hearing.

Joining Felix for the trial were the high priest Ananias, some

Jewish elders, and an attorney named Tertullus, who was very ready to present a case against Paul. As had happened before, the accusations made against Paul were untrue, and he eloquently offered his rebuttal, answering each lie with truth. As he spoke in his own defense, though, Paul also interwove the gospel message. This man never stopped preaching!

Challenge: When has God delivered you in an unexpected if not miraculous way? Also, when has God brought good—your good and/or kingdom good—from a time of suffering? Our willingness to see our suffering from God's perspective and in light of His purposes can fuel in us hope and peace rooted in knowing that He is at work.

DAY 58

NO FEAR

Do not be frightened or dismayed, for the
LORD your God is with you wherever you go.
Joshua 1:9

Tertullus made his false accusations, Paul defended himself with truth, and Governor Felix listened to both sides. Rather than making a decision right then, Felix adjourned the hearing with the comment, "Wait until Lysias, the garrison commander, arrives. Then I will decide the case" (Acts 24:22 NLT). Felix put Paul in prison but allowed friends to visit and take care of his needs.

Wanting to learn more about faith in Jesus, Felix sent for Paul a few days later. Paul "discussed justice, self-control, and the coming judgment" (Acts 24:25)—and that last topic frightened Felix. Instead of accepting the truth about Jesus as Messiah and pursuing a relationship with Jesus, Felix chose to turn from the invitation to true and eternal life and told Paul, "Go away for the present; when I have an opportunity, I will send for you" (v. 25). Hoping Paul would offer him a bribe to get out of prison, Felix sent for Paul often.

Wanting to gain favor with the Jewish people, Felix left Paul in prison for two years, never deciding on Paul's guilt or innocence. Then Porcius Festus succeeded Felix.

Three days after arriving in Caesarea, Festus headed to Jerusalem to hear about this Paul. There, he encountered the same Jewish leaders still accusing Paul two years later. After staying about a week, Festus returned to Caesarea where he wanted to hear from Paul. Those Jewish leaders from Jerusalem also made the trip to Caesarea to again make accusations about Paul that could not be proved.

No more decisive than Felix, Festus asked Paul if he was willing to stand trial in his Jerusalem court. Sounding frustrated with this Caesarean waste-of-time approach to justice, Paul appealed to Caesar. His appeal was granted.

Challenge: Are you frightened of the day of judgment? About the power of the government? About the unfairness of life? What biblical truths can you speak to yourself to counter your fear?

DAY 59

JUST BELIEVE?

I believe; help my unbelief!
Mark 9:24

Paul was imprisoned for over two years as the indecisive Felix and Festus refused to issue a verdict. Now, since Paul had asked to stand trial before Caesar, Festus needed to be able to "[specify] the charges against him" (Acts 25:27). So Festus called Paul to speak to King Agrippa and his sister, Bernice, in hopes of finding something to write to the emperor.

Yet after listening to Paul's detailed testimony, everyone involved agreed that Paul was innocent: "This man is doing nothing to deserve death or imprisonment" (Acts 26:31). Agrippa added, "This man could have been set free if he had not appealed to the emperor" (v. 32). More than two years after the Lord had made the promise that Paul would go to Rome, he was on his way. The manner and circumstances could not have been what Paul had anticipated, but he was indeed off to Rome.

Paul boarded a ship to Rome in the custody of Julius, a Roman officer and captain of the Imperial Regiment. The voyage was neither smooth nor uneventful. A violent storm arose. The crew made desperate attempts, relying on everything they humanly knew to do, first allowing the ship to be driven along, next, throwing cargo overboard, and then throwing the ship's tackle overboard. Having not eaten for a long time, the travelers finally gave up all hope when "neither sun nor stars appeared for many days," and the storm raged on (Acts 27:20).

As Paul's traveling companion Luke noted, "All hope of our being saved was at last abandoned" (Acts 27:20).

Challenge: When has God fulfilled a promise in a way you never would have imagined? God's ways are best, even though we sometimes don't understand.

When have you lost hope as the storms of life raged on? What did you learn from that experience?

You may be without hope now. Find people in your life who will believe on your behalf right now and pray for you faithfully. And maybe you yourself can muster, "I believe; help my unbelief."

TINA C. ELACQUA, PH.D.

DAY 60

SPIRITUALLY ANCHORED

We have this hope, a sure and
steadfast anchor of the soul.
Hebrews 6:19

The waters were churning, the winds were howling, the ship was being blown along wherever the northeaster pushed it, and the passengers and crew had abandoned hope. But God had spoken to Paul through an angel: "Do not be afraid, Paul; you must stand before the emperor, and, indeed, God has granted safety to all those who are sailing with you" (Acts 27:24). God didn't provide details about the how or the when. God simply told Paul to not be afraid.

In order to believe such promises, we have to know God, His character, His ways, and His thoughts. When we invest in our relationship with Him, we'll be more firmly anchored when the storms of life come.

Anchored spiritually, Paul trusted God as he was blown about on this dark, stormy sea, and he trusted God on behalf of the 276 exhausted, hungry, and desperate men onboard. God used Paul to encourage them.

First, Paul reminded the passengers and crew to believe God's promise that they would be safe and, second, to follow God's instruction: "You will all die unless the sailors stay aboard" (Acts 27:31 NLT). This time (in contrast to Acts 27:9–12 when the crew dismissed tentmaker Paul's sailing advice), those in leadership submitted to Paul: the soldiers cut the ropes of the lifeboat and let it drift away.

Then, at Paul's urging, the men ate and felt encouraged. Even more encouraging was the sight of land after 14 days of the hurricane-like storm. But the ship struck a reef when the crew tried to run the ship aground. Seeing the broken stern, the soldiers onboard wanted to kill the prisoners—including Paul—so that none would escape. God intervened: needing to protect Paul, his centurion escort overruled the soldiers. Just as God promised, all 276 voyagers arrived safely on dry land.

Challenge: What about God and His character anchors you during life's storms? Cite at least five specifics.

DAY 61

DELIVERANCE ON MALTA

The LORD is my rock, my fortress, and my deliverer.
Psalm 18:2

True to His promises, God brought all the crew and passengers to safety on an island called Malta, about sixty miles south of Sicily. The people there "showed us unusual kindness," Luke reported in Acts 28:2.

All those shipwrecked men—who had swum to safety or paddled atop planks from the ship—were cold and wet from the rain. Seeing their need to get warm and dry, the people of Malta built a fire. As Paul added to the flames the sticks he had gathered, a poisonous snake—forced out of the bundle of sticks by the heat of the fire—bit him on the hand. Paul "shook off the creature into the fire and suffered no harm" (Acts 28:5).

When the snake bit Paul, the people of Malta immediately concluded he must be a murderer and this snakebite was an act of justice. The people expected him to swell up or suddenly die. After waiting "a long time" and seeing that Paul remained unharmed, the people of Malta changed their minds and decided he must be a god (Acts 28:6). Clearly, they didn't yet know the One True God, yet they had a sense that a deity who invokes justice existed. When that justice didn't play out as expected—when Paul survived— the people concluded that he must be a god because he proved invincible to the snakebite.

But Paul survived because, as eyewitnesses attested, the One True God whom Paul served protected him.

Challenge: Like the people of Malta, what act of unusual kindness could you do for someone? Like Paul gathering sticks for the fire, what act of service could you do this week? And to whom do you give credit when miracles happen? Are you quick to dismiss the event as a coincidence, or do you recognize the One True God at work? Explain why.

DAY 62

HEALINGS AND GRATITUDE

[Jesus] laid his hands on each of them and cured them.
Luke 4:40

God spared Paul's life when the viper bit him, but that was not the only miracle the Almighty did on Malta.

Acts 28 introduces us to a man named Publius, "the leading man of the island" (v. 7). When he hosted Paul and his companions for three days, Paul learned that Publius's father was ill with fever and dysentery. Paul went to see the man. When Paul prayed and—just as his Lord Jesus had—laid hands on him, God healed this man's father.

Hearing about what had happened, all the other sick people on the island went to see Paul. His prayers for their healing certainly acknowledged God's role in no uncertain terms. He might have prayed something like "Almighty God, the One and Only True God for whom nothing is impossible, please heal this man today, for his good and Your glory!"

During Paul's three months on the island of Malta, God used him to heal all the sick on the island. He undoubtedly also did a good deal of gospel preaching as he spent time among the people. No wonder when the time came for Paul to sail, the people of Malta showed their gratitude by supplying the people on the ship with everything they would need.

Challenge: When have you—or someone you know—personally experienced the loving power of Jehovah-Rapha, the God who heals? Offer details about how the Lord worked.

The people of Malta showed their gratitude to Paul for his healing work among them. What is one of your favorite ways to show someone gratitude for kindness? What do you do to express your gratitude to God for His many blessings?

Finally, in what specific ways do you preach the gospel—with or without words—as you do what God has called you to do whether in the home, neighborhood, or workplace?

DAY 63

SAYING, "THANK YOU"

Encourage one another and build up each other.
1 Thessalonians 5:11

"And so we came to Rome" (Acts 28:14). Talk about an anticlimactic statement! God had made this promise two years earlier. Our faithful God—Promise Maker and Promise Keeper—had finally gotten the apostle to Rome. But "And so we came to Rome" is all the writer provides! What was Paul feeling? What was he thinking? What kind of praise did he offer God? What requests did Paul make of God now that an appearance before Caesar was a real possibility?

Luke went on after that starkly simple statement to say that brothers and sisters in Christ had heard that Paul was coming to Rome. Some of these people met Paul and his companions at the Forum, which was about 43 miles from Rome. Others met Paul and his companions at The Three Taverns, about 35 miles from Rome. These brothers in Christ had made the journey, probably on foot, to greet Paul. Paul had never met these people, but "on seeing them, Paul thanked God and took courage" (Acts 28:15).

God is faithful, so let's thank Him. After all, He has provided us a place to live, a bed to sleep in, the ability to pay our bills, food to eat, and freedom to worship Him. Consider His joy when we also gratefully recognize both His faithfulness and the people He used to provide for us, teach us, guide us, and encourage us.

Challenge: We human beings tend to be quick to complain. May we train ourselves to be quick to instead thank both God and thank one another. Focus this week on one of these options and express your gratitude:

- Document times God has moved in your life.
- Tell someone what God has done for you.
- Write a thank-you note. A text or email can still make someone's day, but the old-fashioned way—a note handwritten on nice stationery—is extra special.

DAY 64

RELYING ON GOD

Call to me, and I will answer you.
Jeremiah 33:3

We've been traveling with Paul through the book of Acts, and we've seen quite a range of responses to him and his gospel message. Some people believed and were all in. Others became enraged and even violent in their disbelief. If Paul had relied only on a crowd's affirmation or the number of people raising their hand during the altar call, he might have been discouraged perhaps even to the point of giving up or at least questioning his calling. In addition to those unfavorable responses to the gospel, Paul also experienced flogging, a shipwreck, stoning, and imprisonment. What kept him from raging at God or trudging along weighed down by understandable discouragement?

Paul's secret to avoiding discouragement—to being able to joyfully live for Jesus Christ—was his wholehearted dependence on his Lord. At all times Paul relied on Jesus, so of course he relied on Jesus to meet him in his discouragement and to provide perspective, peace, rejuvenation, hope, and direction.

In doing so, Paul set an example for us. Just as the Lord always met Paul in his discouragement, He will meet us when we are discouraged and turn to Him. So when you're low, call out to Jesus in prayer. Touch bases with a Christian friend who will pray with you and for you. Open God's Word and find comfort. (When you're not discouraged, be reading and studying the Word so you know where to turn when you're down.) Reach out for Christian counsel. Trying to fight discouragement alone is not a wise or very effective strategy.

The Lord speaks to us when we pray, open His Word, gather at church, and are with fellow believers. Cry out to Jesus and rely on Him as Paul did.

Challenge: What keeps you from depending on the Lord even when you're not discouraged? Make a list. Next to each item note what you can do to overcome that obstacle. Which way(s) of going to Jesus might help you with every barrier that keeps you from fully relying on Jesus?

TINA C. ELACQUA, PH.D.

DAY 65

EYES TO SEE

Ears to hear and eyes to see—
*both are gifts from the L*ORD.
Proverbs 20:12 (NLT)

Throughout the book of Acts and no matter how much Paul was persecuted, he persevered in delivering the gospel message. Even imprisoned in Rome, he called together the Jewish leaders, committed as always to sharing the gospel first with Jews when he arrived in a new place. "Great numbers" of Jews did in fact visit Paul where he was under house arrest (Acts 28:23). All day long Paul tried to convince them that the law of Moses and the Old Testament prophets all pointed to the truth that Jesus of Nazareth is their long-awaited Messiah.

The heart of Paul's message was always the same: Jesus died on the cross for our sins and was buried. On the third day, God raised Jesus from the dead. For forty days, more than 500 eyewitnesses—in twelve appearances—saw the risen Jesus. Before ascending to be with God the Father, Jesus promised to send His followers an advocate. On Pentecost this Holy Spirit arrived and filled the believers with power and joy. That same Holy Spirit—who also provided first-century believers with strength, love, comfort, and guidance—provides the same to us today when we name Jesus our Savior and Lord.

Yet after hearing Paul's message, only some Jews were convinced. Others refused to believe, and Paul left those spiritually blind and deaf people with this:

The Holy Spirit spoke the truth to your ancestors when he said through Isaiah the prophet:

> "'Go to this people and say,
> "You will be ever hearing but never understanding;
>   you will be ever seeing but never perceiving."
> For this people's heart has become calloused;
>   they hardly hear with their ears,
>   and they have closed their eyes.
> Otherwise they might see with their eyes,
>   hear with their ears,
>   understand with their hearts
> and turn, and I would heal them.'" (Acts 28:25–27 NIV)

Challenge: What keeps people blind and deaf to the gospel truth about Jesus? What can believers do to keep their eyes open and their hearts soft toward Jesus?

DAY 66

BEWARE OF COUNTERFEIT TEACHERS!

There will be false teachers among you,
who will secretly bring in destructive opinions.
2 Peter 2:1

Passion and perseverance characterized Paul's faithful preaching of the gospel, first to the Jews and then to the Gentiles. Even under house arrest, Paul boldly proclaimed the gospel news, the good news, about Jesus the Messiah— "and no one tried to stop him" (Acts 28:31 NLT).

In addition to preaching during his first imprisonment in Rome, Paul also wrote letters to the Colossians, the Ephesians, Philemon, and the Philippians. The letter to believers in Colossae, the first letter we'll look at, warns us to be discerning so we don't end up believing deceptive teaching and false doctrine.

In Colossae, people were believing a message that combined elements of paganism and secular philosophy with Christian doctrine. Colossians 2:9–10 is a key verse countering this false teaching: "In [Jesus Christ] the whole fullness of deity dwells bodily, and you have come to fullness in him, who is the head of every ruler and authority." Many religions such as Islam and Jehovah's Witnesses recognize Jesus as a prophet and teacher. But they don't acknowledge that He is Messiah, and acceptance of that fact is key to forgiveness of sins and eternal life.

Paul asserted that when we have named Christ our Savior and

Lord, we have what is necessary for salvation and right living. Being grounded in biblical doctrine also helps lead us to right relationship with the Father, Son, and Spirit; to right living on earth; and to eternal life with God. Both knowing Jesus well and knowing about Him can help us recognize and stand strong against false teachings. What individuals say about Jesus Christ reveals the truthfulness or the deceptiveness of their message. A teaching is false if it asserts that Jesus is anything other than God incarnate, God made flesh. Always look closely at what a teacher says about who Jesus is.

Challenge: What do you do to confirm the teachings and preachings you hear? What do you do to be sure you continue to grow in your knowledge of and relationship with Jesus?

TINA C. ELACQUA, PH.D.

DAY 67

STRENGTH FOR THE BATTLE

Be strong in the Lord and in his mighty power.
Ephesians 6:10 (NIV)

Paul's words in Colossians offer the crucial warning to be on guard and not fall for deceptive teachings and false doctrine. Paul also wrote to believers in Ephesus where people around them were interested in the unseen world and the supernatural. Fascinated by wizardry, sorcery, witchcraft, and astrology as some people today are, some individuals—then and now—ended up pursuing Satan instead of Jesus. These occult practices are forbidden by God (see Deuteronomy 18:10–11), and Satan is the power behind these activities. If you find yourself intrigued by the possibility of knowing the future, remember that God tells us all we need to know about the future in His Word. Stay focused on Scripture and on your relationship with the One who knows the future and is sovereign over it.

Well aware of Satan's power, Paul also addressed the matter of spiritual warfare. Appropriately called the Father of Lies, our deceitful enemy, tries to trick us and to lure us away from God. Yet, as Paul reminded us, we are not alone when Satan and his minions attack. God Himself helps us take a "stand against the wiles of the devil" (Ephesians 6:11). The apostle Paul exhorted us to "be strong in the Lord and in the strength of his power" (v. 10). In addition, we human beings are limited in our discernment, wisdom, and strength, but God is not. The Creator of the heavens and earth and the sovereign Ruler of everything is all powerful. Furthermore, His Holy Spirit—"who raised Jesus from the dead" (Romans 8:11 esv)—dwells within believers, empowering us when we call on Him.

We are strong when we abide in the Lord and rely on Him.

Challenge: Tell what happened one time when you called on the Lord for strength in a spiritual battle. Also, share what you do to abide in the Lord and thereby fuel your strength for battles against the Father of Lies.

DAY 68

THE ARMOR OF GOD

Take up the whole armor of God, that you may be able to withstand in the evil day, and having done all, to stand firm.
Ephesians 6:13 (ESV)

We learn in Ephesians that in addition to providing us with His indwelling Holy Spirit who gives us strength for battles against the enemy, God also provides us with His armor. And Paul was clear: in order to stand against the schemes of the devil, we must put on the *whole* armor of God (Ephesians 6:13, emphasis added). We need all that God provides us because our enemy is evil, deceptive, and powerful:

> Our struggle is not against blood and flesh but against the rulers, against the authorities, against the cosmic powers of this present darkness, against the spiritual forces of evil in the heavenly places. (v. 12)

We can forcefully resist those "spiritual forces of evil" and refuse the devil's temptations when we take up the six pieces of armor God has given us:

Belt of truth
Breastplate of righteousness
Shoes that are the gospel of peace
Shield of faith

Helmet of salvation

Sword of the Spirit, God's Word (see vv. 14–18)

That's quite the suit of armor, isn't it? In prayer, be sure to put it on each day. Build that into your morning routine. Then, once you have it on, be "praying at all times in the Spirit" (v. 18 ESV). God will not only protect you with His armor, but He is there through prayer to strengthen you and guide you.

Challenge: Look again at the pieces of armor and then think back over your week. Which piece of armor might have been—or if you were wearing it, which piece was—helpful in a specific situation? Describe the circumstances and the effect or potential effect of the armor.

DAY 69

THE GRACE OF FORGIVENESS

In [Jesus] we have redemption through his blood, the forgiveness of our trespasses, according to the riches of his grace.
Ephesians 1:7

Philemon is a curious little letter. The apostle Paul was writing to Philemon, a man who lived in Colossae, a man whom Paul had led to Christ and who had been a partner in ministry.

Although he might have used his authority and put pressure on Philemon, Paul simply made an appeal. He asked Philemon to forgive his runaway slave, Onesimus, and accept him back not as a slave, but as a brother in Christ because he had become a true believer.

In his next statement, Paul made Philemon an offer that reflects what our Savior and Redeemer has done. Paul said, "If [Onesimus] has wronged you at all, or owes you anything, charge that to my account.... I will repay it" (Philemon 1:18–19 ESV). Paul was willing to follow the pattern of redemption that Christ showed us when He redeemed us from the consequences of our sin: God forgives our sin and welcomes us into His family as His children. Because of Christ's death as the perfect sacrifice for our sin and His resurrection victory over sin and death, God sees believers as blameless. Jesus paid the debt we owed God, and Paul was willing to pay any debt Onesimus owed Philemon.

In addition to showing us a picture of forgiveness, the letter to Philemon also speaks of the power of the gospel to transform a person's life. These 25 verses are a call to forgiveness and a picture of God's redeeming grace.

Challenge: To whom—if anyone—do you need to extend forgiveness? Know that you can extend forgiveness even if the person doesn't ask for forgiveness. God's command to forgive is a command for your good. Your heavenly Father wants you to be free of the burden of hurt and anger, the burden of wanting revenge, and any seed of bitterness. Talk to God about the person you need to forgive and see what He does in your heart.

DAY 70

JOY IN SUFFERING

*Whenever you face various trials, consider it all joy, because
you know that the testing of your faith produces endurance.*
James 1:2–3

During his first imprisonment in Rome, Paul wrote to the
Colossians, the Ephesians, Philemon, and—the letter we'll look
at today—the Philippians. On Paul's second missionary journey,
he and his companions started the church in Philippi, the very
first church on the European continent.

A well-known verse—and tough command—is Philippians
4:4, "Rejoice in the Lord always; again I will say, Rejoice." A form
of the words *rejoicing* and *joy* appears many times in this book as
Paul addressed what the NRSV describes as joy in suffering, joy
in serving, joy in believing, and—my edit!—joy in being content.
And perhaps the first in Paul's list is the most counterintuitive
and challenging. How do we choose joy when we're struggling,
hurting, and suffering—and why would we even make that choice?

Remember that Paul—who had also been shipwrecked,
flogged, stoned, left for dead, hungry, thirsty, and discouraged—
wrote to the Philippians while he was in prison. Paul had learned
to choose joy whatever his circumstances, and he did so by
focusing on Jesus Christ as the provider of that joy. He trusted
God to always be using the suffering for good: "Everything that
has happened to me here has helped to spread the Good News. For

everyone here, including the whole palace guard, knows that I am in chains because of Christ" (Philippians 1:12–13 NLT).

Setting a solid example for us, Paul focused on the truth of God's sovereignty. He believed in God's ongoing oversight of both circumstances universal and his own personal circumstances, an oversight that meant the fulfillment of His kingdom purposes for world history and for each of His children. May we, like Paul, learn to trust in the Lord's sovereign hand over every aspect of our life and choose joy.

Challenge: Tell of a time when you—or someone you know or know about—genuinely knew joy in suffering. Explain why you think that was possible.

DAY 71

JOY IN SERVING

*In your relationships with one another, have
the same mindset as Christ Jesus:
Who… made himself nothing
by taking the very nature of a servant.*
Philippians 2:5–7 (NIV)

Quoting an early Christian hymn in Philippians 2, Paul shared that the key to our knowing joy when we serve is having the attitude and mind of Christ. Jesus came in humility to serve, and His ultimate act of service was dying on the cross for our sin.

Serving happens not only on the monumental scale of Christ's sacrificial death. Serving happens on a big scale, yes, but also—from our merely human perspective—on a so-called small scale, yet God is honored and glorified in every single one of the wide-ranging ways we serve Him.

Imagine being able to serve as the president of a nonprofit, from a key government position, or through a strong presence as a teaching pastor whose messages have an international reach. In God's economy, that service is no more valued than serving the Lord by changing diapers and feeding a family; by working with excellence in an entry-level position or a volunteer capacity; or by ushering at church and preparing Sunday school crafts.

Sometimes we serve voluntarily: we sign up to chaperone a high-school retreat; we open our home to a friend in need; or we anonymously leave a bag of groceries for a family we know could use it.

Sometimes, though, nothing about the task feels like God-glorifying service. That's when we need to—as the title of Brother Lawrence's little book says—*Practice of the Presence of God* "by continually conversing with Him" while we're meeting deadlines, holding babies in the church nursery, and, as Lawrence did, peeling potatoes and washing dishes. After all, he pointed out, God "regards not the greatness of the work, but the love with which it is performed."

Challenge: When have you felt genuine joy while serving? Describe what you were doing and share ideas about why it was joyful. Consider, too, why you did or didn't expect to experience that joy.

DAY 72

JOY IN BELIEVING

I count everything as loss because of the surpassing worth of knowing Christ Jesus my Lord.
Philippians 3:8 (ESV)

As we've seen, Paul chose to know joy in suffering, and he also knew the joy of serving. Today we'll look at the joy this apostle found in believing.

When we first met Paul in Acts 7:58, he was watching the apostle Stephen be stoned. His silent approval was chilling. Completely blind to the gospel truth about who Jesus was and His place in God's redemptive plan for all of humanity, Paul was "ravaging the church," arresting believers, men and women alike, and throwing them in prison (8:3). When he was "still breathing threats and murder against the disciples of the Lord" (9:1), Paul recognized the gospel truth about Jesus, the Lamb of God, and his radical transformation began (see Acts 9:1–30; 22:1–21 and Galatians 1:11–24).

I would imagine that Paul's experience aligned with the words of the classic hymn: "I once was blind, but now I see." Joy in believing comes with seeing eternal-life-giving truth after living in darkness. Joy in believing comes with understanding grace when we had once been legalistically following rules to earn acceptance, and joy comes with recognizing that being in a personal relationship with God is His intention, not a matter of following rules.

God's amazing grace enables us first to recognize Jesus as His Son, our Savior. But His grace then defines our walk with Him, bringing us guidance, hope, peace, and, yes, joy.

Challenge: Reflect on your experience of once being blind to gospel truth and then being able to see the love of God for you evident in the sacrificial life and death of Jesus. What joy did you find in believing initially? What joy in your faith have you experienced since then? Share a few examples of joy that have been especially encouraging and life-giving.

DAY 73

JOY IN BEING CONTENT

I have learned to be content with whatever I have.
I know what it is to have little, and I know
what it is to have plenty.
Philippians 4:11–12

Read again Paul's bold statement and know that you and I can learn to be content even as Paul did. Key to contentment is yielding ourselves—heart, soul, mind, spirit, dreams, hopes—to God, trusting that He who knows best has allowed our circumstances for His glory and good purposes.

Philippians 4:6 says, "Do not be anxious about anything, but in everything by prayer and supplication with thanksgiving let your requests be made known to God." The Greek for *supplication* invites us to take our personal needs to God. We can pray specifically, personally, and with thanksgiving, inviting the Lord's will to be done in the circumstances that don't naturally give rise to joy. As we surrender to the Lord our worries, anxieties, and fears, we can know the joy that comes with being content in Him.

Paul continued in Philippians 4: "I can do all things through him [Christ] who strengthens me" (v. 13). Relying on the Lord's strength and depending on Him for direction and wisdom can also help us deal with the lack of contentment prompted by situations or relationships.

Another key to finding contentment is to choose to focus our thoughts on "whatever is true, whatever is honorable, whatever is just, whatever is pure, whatever is lovely, whatever is commendable, if there is any excellence, if there is anything worthy of praise, think about these things" (Philippians 4:8 ESV). God Himself meets all these criteria, and thinking about Him will ground us in the contentment of knowing we are His beloved child. Can there be a greater reason for contentment and the joy it brings?

Challenge: Joy in suffering, joy in serving, joy in believing, joy in being content: these come together as joy in Jesus. Identify one or two significant teachings about joy from today's reading and/ or the three previous ones. What will you do to live out these teachings about joy?

DAY 74

BEFORE AND AFTER

If anyone is in Christ, there is a new creation: everything old has passed away; look, new things have come into being!
2 Corinthians 5:17

When Paul was released from house arrest in Rome—freedom he enjoyed for a few years—he wrote 1 Timothy and Titus. Then during his last imprisonment, he wrote 2 Timothy. These three books offer much to us even today, and we'll consider a key theme from 1 Timothy.

Paul recognized God's mercy on him and was grateful for it. Despite persecution, shipwrecks, imprisonments, hunger, stoning, being whipped, and being beaten, Paul remained thankful that God chose him to lead others to Christ. Hear the apostle's own words:

> I am grateful to Christ Jesus our Lord, who has strengthened me, because he considered me faithful and appointed me to his service, even though I was formerly a blasphemer, a persecutor, and a man of violence. But I received mercy because I had acted ignorantly in unbelief, and the grace of our Lord overflowed for me with the faith and love that are in Christ Jesus. The saying is sure and worthy of full acceptance: that Christ Jesus came into the world to save sinners—of whom I am the foremost.

But for that very reason I received mercy, so that in me, as the foremost, Jesus Christ might display the utmost patience as an example to those who would come to believe in him for eternal life. To the King of the ages, immortal, invisible, the only God, be honor and glory forever and ever. Amen. (1 Timothy 1:12–17).

Amen! And hallelujah!

Challenge: Take a few minutes to think about the person you were before you met Jesus; the mercy God has shown you; and how He wants to use you—just as He used Paul—to help others to come to know Christ. Act on what He shows you about His calling to share the gospel.

DAY 75

MAKING PERSONAL THE ACCOUNT OF ACTS

Jesus came and said to them, "All authority in heaven and on earth has been given to me. Go therefore and make disciples of all nations, baptizing them in the name of the Father and of the Son and of the Holy Spirit and teaching them to obey everything that I have commanded you. And remember, I am with you always, to the end of the age."
Matthew 28:18–20

These words of Jesus have come to be known as the Great Commission, and He gave this assignment to His first-century disciples as well as to His disciples since then—and that includes you and me. Maybe you've heard Jesus' marching orders many times before, or maybe they're new to you today. Either way, having completed this study of Acts and many of Paul's letters, you may have a clearer idea of what obedience to this command looks like and of what kingdom-of-God fruit results when we obey it.

What might obedience to Jesus' Great Commission look like in your life? In other words, what actions might you take as you "fight the good fight of the faith" (1 Timothy 6:12)?

Preaching like Peter (Acts 4:8–12)
Serving in the church like Stephen (6:1–10)
Church planting like Paul (14:1–7)
Encouraging like Barnabas (4:36)

Offering hospitality like Lydia (16:14–15)
Selling a possession and giving the proceeds
to the church like Barnabas (4:36–37)
Serving fellow believers by sharing possessions
like the early church (4:32–35)
Praying for the healing of fellow believers like Peter (9:32–34)
Teaching Christian truth like Priscilla and Aquila (18:26)
Having a leadership role in church like James (15:13–21)

Know that whatever form of service God is calling you to perform in response to the Great Commission during this season of your life, He will enable you to fulfill that purpose. To Him be the glory!

Challenge: What do you sense God wants you to do in response to the Great Commission? What keeps you from wholehearted, full-throttled obedience to Jesus' Great Commission? Be specific about the barriers, whether they're emotional, mental, circumstantial, or something else. Ask God to give you wisdom about how to remove or get past those barriers—and remember that Jesus is "with you always, to the end of the age."

FINISHING WELL

Let us run with perseverance the race that is set before us,
looking to Jesus, the pioneer and perfecter of faith.
Hebrews 12:1–2

As we finish up *Fight the Good Fight: 75 Days of Growing Closer to Jesus,* I hope you have come to understand and respect Paul the apostle and—even more important—to know better and love more deeply Jesus Christ, your Savior and Lord.

As someone who was sold out to Jesus, committed to follow Him whatever the personal cost, Paul gave us a compelling example to follow. He set the bar high because our God deserves us to be the best representatives of His rock-solid truth, His servant heart, and His gracious, transforming love.

Hear, for instance, Paul's call to right living: "Renounce impiety and worldly passions... to live lives that are self-controlled, upright, and godly, while we wait for the blessed hope and the manifestation of the glory of our great God and Savior, Jesus Christ" (Titus 2:12–13). Act on whatever God is saying to you personally in these verses. Your obedience to this command—to all of His commands—will benefit you as it makes you shine brighter for Him.

Then, shortly before his death, Paul wrote down this glorious promise: "The Lord will deliver me from every evil attack and will bring me safely into his heavenly Kingdom" (2 Timothy 4:18 NLT). In Nero's Rome Paul died a violent death, but as his writing reveals, he faced that inevitable moment with complete confidence that God would take him safely into His heavenly kingdom. If you aren't fearlessly facing death, don't stay in that spot. Turn to Scripture, a pastor, or a fellow believer for reassurance.

Finally, consider adopting these breathtaking words from the apostle Paul as a purpose statement for your life:

> I have fought the good fight, I have finished the race, and I have remained faithful. And now the prize awaits me—the crown of righteousness, which the Lord, the righteous Judge, will give me on the day of his return. (2 Timothy 4:7–8 NLT)

As you live by God's grace and according to truth you discovered in our study of Acts and many of Paul's letters, may you, too, fight the good fight and finish strong!

God bless you!
Tina

ACCEPTING JESUS' INVITATION TO SALVATION

Acting with mercy, love, and power, God transformed Paul from persecutor to evangelist—and God wants to transform us as well. Whatever our past, nothing we've done or said can disqualify us from entering God's welcoming embrace. God sent His Son to pay for our sins, however many and however heinous, and Jesus did exactly that when He died on the cross. When we accept that truth, God invites us into relationship with Him so we can receive His transformative love and so He can use us to share with others His love and the truth about Him.

The Romans Road to Salvation*

1. The Diagnosis of Humanity
All have sinned and fall short of the glory of God. Romans 3:23

There is no one who is righteous, not even one. Romans 3:10

The wages of sin is death. Romans 6:23

2. Our Desperation
Wretched person that I am! Who will rescue me from this body of death? Romans 7:24

3. The Decision We Face
If you confess with your mouth that Jesus is Lord and believe in your heart that God raised him from the dead, you will be saved. For with the heart one believes and is justified, and with the mouth one confesses and is saved. Romans 10:9–10 (ESV)

4. Our Deliverance
God proves his love for us in that while we still were sinners Christ died for us. Romans 5:8

The free gift of God is eternal life in Christ Jesus our Lord. Romans 6:23

Everyone who calls on the name of the Lord shall be saved. Romans 10:13

5. God's Grace
Since we have been justified by faith, we have peace with God through our Lord Jesus Christ. Through him we have also obtained access by faith into this grace in which we stand, and we rejoice in hope of the glory of God. Romans 5:1–2 (ESV)

* Based on Shari Abbott with Reasons for Hope (https://reasonsforhopejesus.com/roads-to-salvation-romans-road-john-revelation/)

The first step on the Romans Road is not merely reading through those five essential facts but being sure you understand them and then accepting them as truth. By definition, though, you and I take a step of faith without having all the answers. Know that answers come—or sometimes certain questions become less important—as you walk with Jesus and get to know Him better.

The next step is letting God know of your new commitment to Him. Below is a prayer that can help you do exactly that:

> God, I know that I have sinned against you and am deserving of punishment. But Jesus Christ took the punishment that I deserve so that through faith in Him I could be forgiven. With your help, I place my trust in You for salvation. Thank You for Your wonderful grace and forgiveness – the gift of

eternal life! Amen! (https://www.gotquestions.org/
Romans-road-salvation.html)

Now your journey can really begin! Get a copy of the Bible
(the primary versions I use are the New Revised Standard, the
English Standard Version, and the New Living Translation) and
start getting to know Jesus by reading Mark and Luke, Matthew
and John. Try to read for five or ten minutes a day, beginning by
asking God to show you what He wants you to see in the day's
reading.

Also, find a local church that you can attend regularly, a
church where you can learn, study, and spend time with others
who are journeying through life with Jesus as their Savior and
Lord. Ideally, you'll know a Christian or two who can help you
find a solid, Bible-based church.

God bless you on this life-giving and eternal-life-giving
adventure with Jesus!

LEARN MORE ABOUT TINA AND LISA

About Tina:

Dr. Tina Elacqua is a disciple of Jesus Christ and president of Doral Cove Ministries. Tina has dedicated her life to encouraging and comforting others with truth from God's Word. Having experienced personal tragedy and adversity, Tina recognizes that these hardships yielded the unexpected and beautiful gift of knowing that God's infinite love will mend the most broken of hearts and that faith in Him will unburden the weariest of souls. Tina uses her spiritual gifts to minister to and uplift women, to guide them through thick darkness to a place of light, hope, freedom, and joy, and to help them experience that with God "all things are possible" (Matthew 19:26).

A university psychology and business professor for more than 30 years, Tina holds a Ph.D. from Central Michigan University in Industrial and Organizational Psychology. She is the author of numerous books and journal articles, including *Hope Beyond Loss, Hope Beyond Homicide: Remembrance Devotionals*, and *Living in Freedom: A Biblical Road Map to Navigating Life's Pain*. Tina's books may be purchased online at www.doralcove.com

Tina and her husband, Laird, reside in Jackson, Tennessee, with their two beautiful daughters, three cuddly cats, and two playful dogs.

About Doral Cove Ministries:

Established in 2012, Doral Cove Ministries offers online Christian resources for people looking to meet Jesus, to strengthen their relationship with our Lord and Savior Jesus Christ, and to help them experience the richness of abiding in Him. The ministry offers a wealth of support, including Bible-based articles, books, media, and seminars that instruct and inspire. If you'd like Dr. Tina Elacqua to speak to your congregation or if you want information about implementing one of her popular ten-week seminars at your church, please visit www.doralcove.com

About Lisa:

Lisa Guest graduated magna cum laude and Phi Beta Kappa from the University of California, Irvine, with a B.A. in English, and she completed her master's degree in medieval literature at UCLA. Through the years, Lisa has written 365-day devotionals and video curricula (script, leader's guide, participant's guide) as well as worship journal articles, book reviews, a magazine cover story, and back cover/catalog copy. She has copyedited and developed companion study guides for some of today's most respected Christian writers. Her involvement in the publishing industry combines her love for the written word, her English teacher's eye for errors, and her heart for ministry. Lisa lives in Southern California with her husband, Mike, and they have five adult children, two by marriage.

MORE CHRISTIAN RESOURCES BY DR. ELACQUA

Dr. Tina Elacqua has contributed to the following Christian books. They are available through Amazon (http://amazon.com/author/drtelacqua) and Dr. Elacqua's website at http://www.doralcove.com

Beauty Is Soul Deep: 180 Devotions for Growing a Meaningful Inner Life

Hope Beyond Loss

Hope Beyond Homicide: Remembrance Devotionals

Living in Freedom: A Biblical Road Map for Navigating Life's Pain

Shared Encouragement: Inspiration for a Woman's Soul

Today, God Wants You to Know (also available in Spanish)

365 Devotional Readings for Wives: To Love and to Cherish

365 Daily Whispers of Wisdom for Busy Women

365 Daily Whispers of Wisdom for Mothers of Preschoolers

Printed in the United States
by Baker & Taylor Publisher Services